Reading The Book Of Nature

Reading The Book Of Nature

A Phenomenological Study of Creative Expression in Science and Painting

Edwin Jones

Ohio University Press
Athens

Ohio University Press books are printed on acid-free paper. ∞

LIBRARY OF CONGRESS
Library of Congress Cataloging-in-Publication Data

Jones, Edwin, 1942–
Reading in the book of nature : a phenomenological study of creative expression in science and painting / Edwin Jones.
p. cm. — (Series in continental thought : 14)
Bibliography: p.
ISBN 0–8214–0908–5
1. Creation (Literary, artistic, etc.) 2. Creative ability.
3. Aesthetics. 4. Phenomenology. 5. Galilei, Galileo, 1564–1642.
6. Husserl, Edmund, 1859–1938. 7. Heidegger, Martin, 1889–1976.
8. Cézanne, Paul, 1839–1906. I. Title. II. Series.
BH301.C84J66 1988
128′.3—dc19 88–13092
CIP

Dedicated to

My parents, Mildred and Edwin Jones,
whose support for my studies has endured
beyond all reason

And to E. F. K.
in admiration and friendship

Tallahassee, Florida
9 December 1985

CONTENTS

CHAPTER 1

Introduction: The Paradox of Creativity

Bevor "gedacht" wird, muss schon "gedichtet" worden sein. -NIETZSCHE[1]

At the outset an investigation of creative expression is faced with paradox. In order for any gesture, or resulting artifact, to communicate significantly, a community of perceiving subjects is required—a community subtended by a shared world whose general horizon and basic structures are held in a common understanding. The shared conception of such a world—the common "meaning horizon," or "horizon of significance," as I shall call it, intending thereby to suggest the integration of its structure as well as the implicit character of its incorporation in a body of beliefs—is the required ground on which a gesture or artifact may stand forth as an expressive figure, the shared context wherein it may be mutually understood. Yet in order for an expression to be creative, to be *"gedichtet"* in Nietzsche's phrase, so that something may be *"gedacht,"* it may not simply pass along inherited meanings, even newly arranged; for its originality would then be mere difference, idiosyncrasy, or oddity, rather than genuine invention. At best it would be the first realization of a permutation already prefigured in the total store of meanings associated with the structures of the familiar world. As creative, the expressive gesture must institute new meanings, even while making these significant in relation to the old; in doing so it will bring forth a newly integrated meaning horizon, rooted in but not prefigured by the old structure.

Hence the paradox: Expression is dependent upon a commonly understood world, or familiar meaning horizon; yet as creative it can neither remain as inherited within that world nor find its norm there. If Nietzsche is to be believed, it has the task of inventing its own world, the structure of which exhibits its own norm. Creative expression, then, must originate its own aim and establish its own context of significance; yet for such an achievement to signify at all, it must do so in relation to a pregiven horizon, which will itself be changed and given a new clarity, hence a new communal effectiveness, by virtue of having been brought to expression.

For the most part everyday communication operates with available meanings grounded in the already familiar structures of the shared world and manipulates these in common or standardized patterns to call forth what is already understood. Such communication thus exhibits what Heidegger called *Gerede:* idle talk, which merely passes along available meanings, trading them in ritualistic fashion within a commonly understood context. This kind of talk, as ritual either formally or informally constituted and maintained, has its proper usefulness. It gets us coffee in the café, seats at the ballpark, and a partner to stand with us before the priest or preacher whose own talk binds us together "till death or divorce do us part." This manner of talk, however, derives its expressive and effective powers from what is already understood and remains within the horizon of that prior understanding. Such "constituted speech," as Merleau-Ponty calls it, "assumes that the decisive step of [authentic] expression has [already] been taken."[2] It cannot establish, in the first instance, the meanings and meaning horizon on which it depends. This characteristic dependency indicates that idle talk is talk that has become idle, that is, separated from the originary speech that in opposition is called *Rede* by Heidegger, and *Gedicht* by Nietzsche.

Once a distinction is made between meanings already possessed and their rearrangement in novel contexts to create new meanings, a distinctive problem has been localized that presents itself in one of two guises: either how authentic speech becomes idle or, on the reverse side, how a new significance may be said to accrue to concepts already possessed. With its two sides, the single problem set by the paradox of creative expression calls for a resolution that will itself exhibit a dual motion. On the one hand, it involves tracing available, sedimented meanings back to an originary act of expression that has already been grounded in an experience of those significances held in common by subjects inhabiting a shared world. On the other hand, it involves an attempt to capture that movement in which a personally felt significance is transferred into an expressive structure and thus transformed into a *signification,* that is, the movement whereby metaphor conveys a thought and makes it available for later operations, for a community of subjects.[3]

Thus, even though the problem divides into two phases, it remains one; the two phases are essentially related, for each leads into the other. On one side, the meanings readily available to everyday speech are grounded in an implicit understanding of a structural whole, namely the shared horizon of significance; on the other, an originary act of expression, likewise grounded in an implicit understanding but now personally experienced as a "felt significance," articulates that structural whole and makes it explicit in a publicly accessible artifact, thereby establishing the norms of a newly integrated meaning horizon within which new meanings become available.

In order to follow out this circle of interpretation, and to elucidate the crucial linkage between its two phases, it will be necessary to describe certain meaningful structures within the totality of experience that, although vital to conceptual thought and linguistic convention, are themselves found in a stratum of experience that is neither purely conceptual nor primarily linguistic. These structures, which are overlooked in everyday speech, also are ignored, and indeed on principle, by traditional causal and psychological strategies for explaining human creativity, owing in part to the influence of conceptual and linguistic analysis, and further to the characterization of objective-scientific criteria as the only acceptable norms for establishing the validity of meanings.

In general, the stratum of experience broached in an account of creative expression does not lend itself to strictly objective-scientific modes of analysis, although that does not mean it escapes all manner of "rational" investigation. It does mean, however, that the descriptions by which such experience is recalled require a vocabulary not found in everyday speech, nor indeed in scientific discourse. If for that reason some of the terms in the following descriptions at first seem rather unusual or strange, it should be noted that they belong to a tradition that is already well established, if not generally familiar, namely the recent phenomenological movement in philosophy. We need only keep in mind that such terminology, perhaps as odd or "technical" in the original German and French as in English, is intended solely to discriminate matters not picked out by more customary vocabulary. Here in particular, these matters are structures of experience that we all have, that are pervasively "present" in our lives, and that are meaningful even though retaining their nonconceptual and nonlinguistic nature.

The importance of such *structures* is, perhaps, worth stressing, for they are what render phenomenological description something other than impressionistic. Indeed, the precedence that description takes over argumentation in the phenomenologist's methodology is based on the insight that human life is animated by structures that are imbued with significance, that are "pregnant with *sens*" as Merleau-Ponty says, but that nevertheless are neither logically nor linguistically shaped; their significance is "prepropositional." As such, they are not to be deduced, but rather uncovered, or "disclosed," by whatever descriptive means the phenomenologist commands. Here, as with any explication, the "proof" lies in our "seeing" the sense of what is laid out. In any given case phenomenological description may go wrong. But then, too, it may subsequently be made right, precisely because it is directed toward, and indeed restrained by, such inherently meaningful structures—as, for example, Husserl's "eidetic structures," Merleau-Ponty's "gestalten," and Heidegger's "existentials," or even, in the case of an aesthetic critic, a work of art.

The structures of experience pertinent to interpreting the phenomenon of creative expression are characterized as "ontological" in Heidegger's preparatory analysis of human existence.[4] In this way he distinguishes them from the "ontical" structures treated in an ontology based on *substance,* such as is exhibited by our ordinary "scientific" descriptions. This distinction serves in part to indicate that the constitutive moments of uniquely human existence must be understood in the first instance as integral wholes, that is, as structures whose significance does not derive from a summation of their parts. They cannot be accounted for in "ontical" analysis, precisely because that approach obscures the structural integrity of the phenomena by giving priority to discrete entities, indeed to "atoms," which are subsequently "added" together.

Because any objective-scientific inquiry, whatever may be its specific domain, is ontical in this sense, that is, it assumes the priority of entities in terms of both "knowing" and "being," an understanding of the presumed totality will be held to derive from a construction, or synthesis of particular entities that, when given in "clear and distinct ideas," are discrete. Complete and systematic attainment of an understanding of the whole must on this approach be indefinitely deferred, if not referred ultimately to the mind of God; or it will be projected as the grasp of a universal concept of the ideal totality of such entities. Yet, the relational structure of the manifold of scientific entities has become presupposed as a heuristic principle; in this way, "the uniformity of nature" constitutes an initial premise for any systematic formulation of general scientific laws. As such, a purely "ontical" inquiry, whether represented by the natural sciences or by a "science of language," cannot account for an originary expression of the required horizon of significance. It leaves our problem not only untouched, but untouchable.

The interest that impels this investigation is to see how a meaning horizon can first emerge, specifically how creative expression brings an implicitly understood horizon into communal effectiveness so as to make new meanings available. This interest will lead to reflections upon the ontological structures of human existence, and thus upon a stratum of experience that does not, and need not, occupy scientists working within the conceptual context already established in their tradition. Such experience cannot receive its proper respect if "physicalistic naturalism" is allowed to prevail as an unquestionable epistemological doctrine. Part of the task here, then, is to see how the presupposition of an objective physical universe, held to be univocally given as valid for all, is an idea that must itself have emerged through an expressive act that gave a new significance to an available concept, and that set the norms for the modern understanding of "Nature."

For example, when the Galilean conception of "Nature" is seen to be the result of an inventive achievement—a *gedacht* made available in a *gedichtet*—it can no longer be unassailably claimed as the general horizon of significance for all communication, as modern everyday speech tends to do by taking the object of natural scientific knowledge to be the meaning of "the world." It will perhaps be useful, then, to reread Galileo, not for scientific insight but rather for prescientific insight, specifically in an effort to identify the prior understanding operative in his achievement of a new meaning horizon in which Aristotelian "philosophy of nature" was replaced by a "science of nature," our contemporary mathematical physics.

Yet even if it becomes clear that Galileo "fathered" modern natural science by giving a new significance to an available concept founded in the earlier Aristotelian tradition, the apparent historical regress suggested by this fact need not trap us. After all even Aristotle had his intellectual antecedents in Plato and the Pre-Socratics. The "prior understanding" at issue here does not lie in history in that way, such that it could be lost in the dim reaches of ever more ancient texts and eventually in unrecorded human experience—experience belonging to others. From the phenomenological perspective, that prior understanding lies rather in the personal experience each of us lives through, whatever intellectual account we might give of that experience.

In the works of Husserl, Merleau-Ponty, and Heidegger, the search for a "primal" horizon of significance cuts along a dimension other than the chronological stream of civilization, although it too is a "historical" dimension. This route, as I shall attempt to make clear, leads into what Husserl described as our own prescientific understanding of the "life-world," and into what Merleau-Ponty called "perceptual consciousness," eventually into those inherent structures of human existence Heidegger called "ontological"—all structures of experience, or of human being, that each of us may, when suitably motivated, recover as his own.

The path projected here carries forward, then, a theme shared by these three thinkers, a theme Paul Ricoeur succinctly described as follows:

> in effect, phenomenology carries out a frontal attack on a conviction belonging to all Galileans. The first truth of the world is not the truth of mathematical physics but the truth of perception; or rather the truth of science is erected as a superstructure upon a first foundation of presence and existence, that of the world lived through perceptually.[5]

If the epistemological and ontological priority of Galilean "Nature" has by now long since been dispelled, at least among phenomenologists, the demonstration bears rehearsing, for it clears the way to a new understanding of human creativity and of the role creative expression plays in the life of culture.

What remains to be elucidated further, perhaps even within the ongoing phenomenological tradition, is the method by which primary significances of "the world lived through perceptually" are to be interpreted in a manner that does not obscure the perceptual immediacy of first-order experience. That is, how are the structures of the perceived world brought to expression in a medium that somehow gets "beneath" the abstractions introduced by the language of mathematics into a scientific conception of "Nature," so as to offer those structures for consideration at the level of "presence and existence"?

In view of this question, tracing the Galilean concept of "Nature" to its historical origins is not enough. The unity of that ontical structure cannot be given to primary experience; it can only be thought and indeed, as Galileo's famous dictum has it, thought solely in the terms of mathematics. If the effort to uncover a direct experience of our "natural" meaning horizon leads to *perception* and to the *perceived world,* these must themselves be considered as they occur in their vital significance, that is, in a prescientific stratum of our own personal experience. Before becoming theoretical constructs of any scientific explanation, perception is lived through, and the perceived world is the significant situation that engages us; and these lived experiences remain accessible as such even when we already possess the abstract concepts needed for an intellectual theory. The problem is to reclaim them in the concrete and sensuous immediacy that marks the perceived world as actual, in contrast to the conceptual models of mathematical physics, which are characterized as either possible or necessary.

Despite the alleged difficulties of "bracketing" our scientific knowledge, of placing in suspense what is "known" as part of our modern heritage, this "change of attitude" is precisely what a phenomenological inquiry requires in order to isolate within personal experience a basis for those conceptual superstructures, including but not limited to the scientific, which, as the products and norms of a people's shared understanding, help bind us into a cultural community.

For an example of expression operating at the required level of intuitive significance we could do worse than follow the lead of Maurice Merleau-Ponty, whose career-long interest in "the primacy of perception" ran parallel to an interest in the struggles and achievements of the painter Paul Cézanne. Clearly the painter is in a position to treat perceptual experience directly; his medium conveys the visible in its visibility. In this regard, and by comparison, the language of mathematics may, with Merleau-Ponty, be called "secondary expression." For this reason it will be worth examining the painter's art, specifically as practiced and understood by Cézanne, in order to determine whether his approach to reading "the book of Nature" can reveal its meaningful structures in a way that provides a basis in primary experience for the conceptual superstructures of scientific understanding. In particular, we must ask, can Cézanne's art teach us how to reclaim our primary experience of space, which in Galileo's geometricizing physics remains a pure concept? As we proceed, we shall be forced to distinguish between *space* as a concept and *spatiality* as a characteristic of a lived world, in order to describe the depth of personal vision that Cézanne, perhaps more successfully than any painter before him, recognized as the "essence" of his medium.

Even though Cézanne's efforts to verbalize an intellectual understanding of his own aims and achievements indicate that he too was burdened with a Galilean preconception of nature's reality, an examination of his art may teach us better than his words what he wished to say when he told Émile Bernard:

> One thing is certain, we should not be content with strict reality, with *trompe-l'oeil.* The transposition that a painter makes, with an original vision, gives to the representation of nature a new interest; *he unfolds, as a painter, that which has not yet been said;* he translates it into absolute terms of painting. That is to say, something other than reality. This, indeed, is no longer shallow imitation.[6]

If Cézanne's paintings lead us to reflections and to interpretations that surely never occurred to him, perhaps they will also enable us to understand the tension between his own primary and secondary modes of expression—that is, between the absolute terms of his art, in which he represented nature as it showed itself to him, and the conventional terms of his inherited language, in which "strict reality" tended to remain an ideal, Galilean concept, such as was exploited in the "realistic" techniques of Renaissance painters.

If, in turn, a phenomenological and ontological interpretation of the doubt about his own creativity, which tormented him to the end of his life, shows his doubt to have been spawned by the tension between the absolute exigency of his own personal art and the relativism of an inherited tradition, it should be possible for us to say what he himself could never quite formulate in words. From there, it may also be possible to reinterpret the relation between artistic expression and scientific conception in general, that is, to produce a program for inverting the Platonic view of this relation that Nietzsche's dictum—before the concept, a metaphor—suggests is necessary for an understanding of human creativity. From this newer perspective, what we have been able to conceive in abstraction from an originary act of expression must already have been created in such acts; the *gedacht* must be founded in and created by the *gedichtet*: concepts, in and by aesthetic expression.[7]

Given the preceding, what allows us to claim that creativity is not merely a poetic or artistic function, but a necessary stage in science and philosophy as well?

The patterns implicit in the changing traditions between Galileo and Peripatetic physics on the one hand, as between Husserl and the positivistic tradition on the other, will yield to the same sort of analysis—focused on the establishment of new meaning horizons by acts of creative expression—as is found in the modification of an intellectual tradition, in particular, the change in phenomenology itself between the techniques and results of a Husserl and a Heidegger, via the transition afforded by Merleau-Ponty's adaptation of his German masters.

If I may be permitted this anachronistic view of the development of phenomenology, I should be provided the tools for an analysis of creativity in science, art, and philosophy itself. And beyond this scope, human culture itself may be brought into a clearer focus, as that which grows from the sedimented meaning structures of an inherited tradition to another context in which novel meanings have been incorporated into a newer tradition of lived significances.

CHAPTER 2

Galileo and the Book of Nature

When thought of in connection with natural science, the notion of creativity is easily and often conflated with that of discovery. Perhaps no harm is done by this confusion, except for the loss of rhetorical precision, so long as we remain within a conceptual context determined by the presupposition of "physicalistic naturalism" and refrain from asking about the epistemological status of this prescientific conception of the world from which science takes its start. Thus we celebrate alike, as creative geniuses, those who have discovered a planet or molecule or particle whose existence and characteristics, once determined, resolve some anomaly, and also those who have discovered a solution to a particularly recalcitrant technical problem or theoretical conundrum encountered in the investigation and explanation of nature. The problems, in each case, are held to be set by objective physical nature, which from the outset is taken for granted as indeed given and not at all dependent upon these discoveries. In the popular view, the "book of Nature" already holds the answers, and scientists, however complex their technology and techniques, are in the business of discovering the ways self-sufficient nature operates.

As a result of its evident progress in gathering and correlating information and in formulating ever more comprehensive theories, the institution of natural science appears to be adequately justified in beginning with the preconception of an objective physical world, so that the status of this preconception is no longer considered to be a theme for serious investigation. Indeed, the preconception itself is not amenable to scientific methods, which themselves have gained a reputation as the epitome of rational inquiry. As a result, the question of the origin of this preconception, taken within a conceptual context determined by "physicalistic naturalism" itself, appears to be a strictly historical matter and, moreover, an issue that has been settled when the achievements of Galileo are acknowledged as the principal representative of the inception of modern scientific methods.

Galileo's reputation as the founder of modern natural science, then, rests primarily on his part in the discovery of methods appropriate to investigating a presupposed physical nature, and on his laying the basis for pursuing such methods independently of any nonscientific authority, in particular the Holy Church. Thus "the father of modern science," too, is acclaimed more for his ingenious, or felicitous, discovery and defense of autonomous scientific techniques than he is for a genuinely creative act.

Yet, when we look to Galileo's texts, taken as marking the transition from a "philosophy of nature" founded in Aristotelian cosmology to an experimental and mathematical "science of nature," what we find is not the report of a discovery and efforts to verify it, but rather the expression of a truly inventive conception and the struggle to establish a new meaning horizon in place of that prevailing in the Medieval tradition.

Because "Galilean Nature" is so deeply ingrained in the modern frame of mind, it is perhaps easier for twentieth-century students to comprehend other historically significant accomplishments of this mathematician-philosopher—the dual title Galileo insisted upon when he left the University of Padua and returned to Florence under the patronage of Duke Cosimo.[1] But these aspects of Galileo's intellectual legacy—the discovering of particular facts about nature, the inception of experimental methods involving careful measurement and geometrical demonstration, the establishment of investigative freedom—however important they may be for the history of science, come to be seen as secondary in light of his originary conception of what natural science was thenceforth to understand as its *investigandum.* This conception established how that region was to be understood; its structure set the norm for all acceptable scientific investigation. In this regard, Galileo's profoundest achievement should be recognized as "prescientific," and also as genuinely creative, for it established a new conceptual context that, on reflection, must be recognized as the result of a leap to a new perspective.

Even though the principal explicit theme of his essays and letters is the defense of a method that combines close observation with necessary demonstration, the arguments he presents for this method reveal an underlying universal conception that cannot in turn be verified by experimental results. The methodological blending of the world as given to sense experience with the apodictic order subsisting among mathematical idealities rests upon a prior understanding in which an immutable correspondence has already been posited between physical nature and mathematics. Without that correspondence, Galileo's geometrical demonstrations would lack their characteristic necessity and universality.

It is this originary conception of physical nature as *mathematized,* and its eventual triumph over Peripatetic cosmology, that opened the way for an inquiry into nature conducted according to experimental methods. As a result, careful measurement and mathematical deduction displaced the Peripatetics' syllogistic deductions from Aristotelian "first principles" as the only genuine means of comprehending the natural world. In the new framework, rather than logically determining how a part of nature must behave, given its type of substance and its essential properties, the first step now is observing what it actually does and arranging situations in which that behavior can be accurately measured and analyzed.

If, in this way, Galileo's program placed the investigation of nature on a new footing, where it was no longer dependent upon the doctrine of substance as the only true being worthy of inquiry, it nevertheless left that inquiry dependent upon another ideal model. Whereas the structure of his concept established the norm for methodological principles constituting a truly experimental science of nature, the mathematical ideality of the concept determined that Galilean Nature must forever remain hidden from view behind a veil of pure concepts, to be approached only indirectly, through the language of mathematics.

In order to see more clearly the prescientific character of Galileo's achievement, that is, to see how it represents the creative expression of a concept that science can neither do without nor formulate in its own principal language, it will be useful to examine certain essential aspects of his underlying conception. As a result, we may also come to see the need for somehow reconnecting this abstract concept, this *gedacht,* with the perceived world by means of a newer understanding of its relation to an act of creative expression, to a *gedichtet.*

The underlying conception of Nature implicit in Galileo's texts indicates a world that is isolated from specifically human concerns, a world that is perfectly ordered according to immutable and universal principles, and finally, a world that is amenable to necessary demonstrations mathematically executed. As isolated from human will, Galilean Nature is inexorable and "cares [not] a whit whether her abstruse reasons and methods of operation are understandable to men."[2]

But at the same time, single events closely observed and properly interpreted can be expected to reveal the law governing an infinity of events, because this Nature is conceived as an orderly whole that is subject throughout to the same laws. And further, as a result of the posited correspondence between Nature and mathematical idealities, these laws may be understood and systematically formulated in a language—that of Euclidean geometry—that Galileo himself had inherited in a thoroughly developed form.

Jointly these three aspects of Galileo's conception constitute an objective, though idealized, world whose explanation must be couched in terms of mathematical "causes" rather than in the language of the Aristotelian four "causes." Even though, taken separately, they may not be entirely original with him, his persuasive expression of the conception in which they are unified is representative of the establishment of a new meaning horizon wherein the search for an understanding of the physical world was freed, not only from piety toward Holy Scripture but also from the equally repressive piety toward Aristotelian thought. But Galileo did not present these aspects thematically; they belong to a conception underlying his explicit concerns. And presumably he did not foresee the full extent to which they eventually would remove the object of science from the reach of personal experience. It will, then, be worth the effort to consider how each of these aspects emerged in the defense of his "new sciences."

The isolation of physical nature surfaces most prominently in Galileo's texts as his strategy for obtaining the independence of scientific investigation from the authority of the Holy Church, the topic of his *Letter to the Grand Duchess Christina.*[3] Seeking here an acceptable basis for separating church and science, he described their respective domains as separate and distinct. Although he deferred to Scripture and its appointed interpreters on matters that pertain to salvation and "to faith or ethics, or which concern the edification of Christian doctrine,"[4] he insisted that "physical conclusions" must not be so deferred. Specifically with regard to the debate over the Copernican system, he maintained that "the mobility or stability of the earth or sun is neither a matter of faith nor one contrary to ethics."[5] This and indeed all physical (natural) conclusions are rather matters in which necessary demonstrations and sense experiences ought to be respected. By carefully restricting the region in which these methods are held to be autonomous, that is, in physical conclusions, he isolated this region from that belonging properly to religious concerns; thus he could claim epistemological independence for science without appearing to usurp the Church's authority. Although this distinction failed to satisfy the Inquisition, surely it satisfied Galileo's own sincere Catholic piety; hence, the separation of domains appears to have been as definite and complete in his own mind as he held it to be in Copernicus's work *On the Celestial Revolutions.*[6]

In light of his cultural situation, this strategy, although immediately unsuccessful, was obviously prudent; yet its consequences, which accompanied his posthumous vindication, reached further than he might have foreseen. Just as his defense against religious authority contained the basis for its later generalization into a defense against all nonscientific authority, his separation of physical nature from matters of faith and salvation likewise contained the basis for a generalization: this one into a thoroughgoing isolation from the realm of what came to be called *Geisteswissenschaften*, and indeed from intuitive experience altogether. "Galileo's contribution was to destroy the intuitive view and replace it by a new one," Einstein has said.[7]

On the new view physical nature is not always what it first appears to be. As Galileo recognized, his "new sciences" enabled him to "derive facts which are not only striking and new but which are often far removed from what we would have imagined."[8] In some instances closer observation, for example, vision enhanced by a telescope, will reveal intuition's error, as it did in the discovery of the moon's irregular surface and in the confirmation of the sun's spherical shape through the study of sunspots. In other cases closer examination, for example, through geometrical reasoning, will disprove what at first glance appears highly probable, as Galileo demonstrated in his consideration of the resistance that solids offer to fracture.[9]

Also, on the new view, physical nature is independent of man's will and desires. "It is not in the power of any created being to make things true or false," he writes to Christina, "for this belongs to their own nature and to the fact."[10] Will and desire have their proper place in the human sciences, where they are effective in the actual development of what is to be investigated. In discussions of points of law and the humanities, for example, he notes that one might rightfully judge a case of reasoning by its plausibility and award the victory to him who excelled in subtle arguments, graceful speech, and authority earned through greater experience. But in the natural sciences this will not do, for here "conclusions are true and necessary and have nothing to do with human will."[11]

As isolated from man's wishes, the nature investigated by the scientist is not of his making, nor is it the result of any created being's will; it is truly a region in which man's entreaty is ineffective. Confronting this preestablished and self-contained nature, man can only passively submit to its truth. He is a spectator who arrived after the fact, that is, after the creation and ordering of the physical universe had been completed; and his only effective activity in regard to this fait accompli is to discover the facts and to accommodate himself to them.

Whereas the object of Galileo's concept is not of man's making, the concept itself must be, precisely because of its character as universal. Galileo conceived of a world capable of endlessly verifying the particular hypotheses of natural science, because perfectly ordered according to universal principles; yet the very universality of this concept determines that its verification must remain an infinitely distant, ideal goal that can only be approached asymptotically. This characteristic alone makes it impossible for his achievement to have been a discovery in the strict sense. Positing the world as a single, universally ordered system of bodies requires a leap beyond what can be uncovered to finite experience. Yet Galileo made the leap and defended it against the Aristotelians of his day—most eloquently in the *Dialogue Concerning the Two Chief World Systems,*[12] in which his spokesman, Salviati, engages in debate with a Peripatetic focused on the Copernican versus the Ptolemaic system of astronomy.

In defending the Copernican view insofar as it "considers the earth to enjoy the same perfection as other integral bodies of the universe,"[13] Galileo dismissed Aristotle's division of nature into two essentially different substances, the celestial and the elemental. This division, he argued, is inconsistent with the view that the world, that is, physical nature, is *perfetto*[14]: whole and complete, as the Peripatetics acknowledged, and also "of necessity most orderly, having its parts disposed in the highest and most perfect order among themselves,"[15] in his own spelling out of the notion of perfection.

Aristotle's distinction between celestial and elemental bodies, Galileo notes, rested on the supposed difference in their natural motions—circular for the celestial and straight for the elemental—and on the attribution of perfection to the circular line, thence to circular motion, and finally to bodies whose motions describe these, and the correlative attribution of imperfection to straight lines, motions, and bodies so moving. From these "principles" Aristotle deduced the properties of ingenerability, incorruptibility, freedom from gravity (heaviness) and from levity for the celestial substances, and the contrary properties for elemental substances. But Galileo, arguing in a manner set by the Peripatetics themselves, demonstrated the inconsistency of this bifurcation with the "principle" of the world's perfection.

It follows from this principle, he argued, that only circular motion is possible for integral bodies movable by nature. For, straight motion, continuing ever farther from its starting point, results in a change of place and, as infinite, never reaches its terminus. Such motion, then, would destroy an established order and therefore could be an appropriate natural motion only in the transition from primal chaos to an ordered creation, for instance, when the Creator installed the planets in their respective orbs. But creation of the perfectly ordered universe is, for Galileo, a fait accompli; and straight motion can no longer be natural or free.[16] It can occur only in the restoration of a body to its natural place (or orbit) from which it could have been removed only by an impressed (that is, unnatural) force. On the contrary, circular motion, even as infinite, always returns on itself and thus freely maintains the perfect order of the whole. Circular motion, therefore, is not peculiar to celestial bodies, but rather belongs to all naturally movable bodies. Thus, he concludes, the deduction of the attributes "generable-ingenerable, alterable-inalterable, divisible-indivisible, etc.," by which Aristotle distinguished these substances is erroneous.[17]

Rather than basing the explanation of observed (and supposed) movements on a classification of merely posited substances and a deduction of their essences, Galileo advocated investigating the actually observed motion of bodies, here, for example, those of the terrestrial globe as well as those of celestial bodies, while "always confining ourselves to strictly natural phenomena."[18]

With the benefit of hindsight available to a modern interpreter, we can see that this investigation has no need for the ideas of substance or essence; indeed, it could not seriously be undertaken while these held sway as the norm for explanation. In place of a deductive method concerned with substances and essences, Galilean Nature demands a method of experimentation as the proper access to it; it demands experimentally determined facts and careful measurements as the basis for deriving its laws, which will then be expressed by functionally coordinated quantities, that is, mathematical formulae. And in place of explanation by final causes, exemplified in "natural philosophy" principally by human welfare, explanation will be couched in terms of mathematical causes. In order to make way for mathematical-experimental norms, the old norms had to be abandoned.[19]

Galileo's debate with the Peripatetics in *Two Chief World Systems* presents his explicit attack on "metaphysical" concepts and procedures in natural science. It is also his most thematic statement of the principle described in modern terms as the uniformity of nature, a principle underlying all inductive reasoning in natural science.[20] But this aspect of his conception of Nature is also evident, implicitly for the most part, in his texts on mechanics and local motion.[21]

Clearly the results of his experiments with simple machines and falling bodies were not taken as merely local results but were held to be generalizable to all such bodies and repeatable under similar circumstances that were sufficiently general in their significant aspects to be arranged anywhere. This generality is illustrated by an amusing reductio Galileo offered against those who would have him believe that ancient Babylonians cooked eggs by whirling them rapidly in a sling. When his report of failure to duplicate the results was countered with the charge that he had not duplicated all the conditions, his response was that the only altered condition was that he was not a Babylonian; hence, the absurdity: the cook's being a Babylonian was the cause of heat in the eggs.[22]

The presupposition of uniformity is so obvious for Galileo in these sciences that it is seldom explicitly mentioned. A rare exception occurs in the account given by Salviati (again speaking for Galileo) of the establishment of a common standard by which to measure velocity and time. In need of a standard that would be understood and accepted by everyone, not only the same for all but also readily available, he says, "the Author [that is, Galileo] considers the velocity of a freely falling body adapted to this purpose, since this velocity increases according to the same law in all parts of the world."[23] For the rest, the universality of his concept of physical nature in these sciences goes without saying.

The most influential and familiar indication of this universality is the application of mathematical and geometrical reasoning to the behavior of physical nature. Although by reputation Galileo's close observations and ingenious means for increasing the accuracy of measurements served as the model for generations of scientists, this influence pales in comparison with the effect of his bold assertion that

> this grand book, the universe, . . . is written in the language of mathematics, and its characters are triangles, circles, and other geometric figures without which it is humanly impossible to understand a single word of it; without these, one wanders about in a dark labyrinth.[24]

This familar dictum announces the central aspect of Galileo's conception of Nature and in the same stroke identifies the required mode of expression for interpreting it: physical nature corresponds to mathematical idealities, and its structure can be articulated only in the language of mathematics.

It is significant that, for the expression of this most critical aspect of his underlying conception, Galileo relied on a poetic device—metaphor. In light of modern analysis of language, it becomes clear that this was not merely a stylistic flourish, even though Galileo's writings consistently exhibit a masterful style and a sensitive appreciation for the beauty of well-written prose. In this instance, however, the connection his metaphor announces between Nature and the language of mathematics is an idea that could not have been expressed so effectively by any other means. Indeed, mathematical language is prevented, by its very nature, from expressing its own relation to anything beyond itself. This is the limitation that formal-logical analysis of language, itself conceived on mathematical models, always runs up against, as Wittgenstein's early analyses have made clear.[25] His effort to surmount this limitation by means of a "picture theory," wherein an isomorphism between the forms of propositions and the forms of states of affairs is sought, requires that a comparison be made and thus implies the initially problematic extralinguistic correspondence. Later efforts led him to other metaphors, such as "language-games," and their contexts, "forms of life"[26]; but these, when intended as explanations of the origin of the correspondence, call for explanations of their own origins in a shared meaning horizon where they can be significant.

Galileo, on the other hand, cleanly sliced through this knot that has been pondered so laboriously in the current century. He announced the required correspondence in a medium readily available, and perhaps the only one capable of doing the job: poetic imagery. Whether he was aware of it or not, this medium, especially the metaphor, like the gesture of pointing, requires a creative response; the reader must leap beyond the bare words in their literal sense, beyond the fixed available meanings, and grasp the new idea disclosed by the new expression. Otherwise the metaphor or pointing gesture fails to communicate. But when it is successful, as Galileo's obviously was, it brings into view a new idea—in this case, the correspondence required by mathematicophysical science, but which that science cannot express in its own principal language.

Galileo's apparent comfort with this mixing of media, with expressing a fundamental scientific principle by means of an unscientific figure of speech, is no doubt an indication that for him scientific matters remained closely connected with the entire realm of human concerns. Clearly science was not yet the self-sufficient force that it has since come to be, and in great part as a result of the influence of his own efforts.

Likewise, he seems never to have questioned the correspondence between physical nature and mathematical idealities so influentially asserted by his metaphor. But clearly he recognized this to be an assumption, and although he readily adopted it, he was aware of the modifications required in the transition from mathematical calculations and geometrical demonstrations to physical objects as experienced.

In the first of the *Two New Sciences,* the justification offered for treating physical objects "in a rigid manner [as if they] belonged to simple and pure mathematics" was the explicitly identified assumption that matter is "unchangeable and always the same," that it is a "constant and invariable property."[27] When Simplicio, the Peripatetic, raised the doubt that scientific demonstrations will hold when applied to the natural world, because they are "mathematical, abstract, and far removed from concrete matter,"[28] Galileo responded with a brief reference to a concrete illustration in the practice of goldsmiths, but then he reverted immediately to geometry: "You are greatly mistaken, Simplicio, because the surface increases directly as the square root of the length, a fact which I can demonstrate geometrically."[29] Presumably he considered the elegance of the demonstration to make it a sufficient reply, for he proceeded to the discussion of companion theorems and other geometrical proofs and nowhere directly confronted the main issue of the objection.

The modifications required in the transition from ideal calculations to experienced nature are stressed in his writings on both mechanics and local motion. In mechanics these appear in his distinction between two points of view: one in which the properties of figures are taken in the absolute sense (*prendere assolutamente*), the other in which the material figure is taken as a "moment or compound force" (*momento o forza composta*).[30] The results of calculations *preso assolutamente* will be ideal and will not coincide precisely with the empirical measurements of a *forza composta.* Likewise, regarding moving bodies he grants that "conclusions proved in the abstract will be different when applied in the concrete."[31] Despite these acknowledged discrepancies, the required corrections can be made, he holds, if one is guided by experience and necessary demonstrations.

It is clear that, for Galileo, mathematical theorems and demonstrations uncover physical nature in its pure precise ideality, but owing to the deviations and difficulties that arise from the human side, *techné* requires the guidance of accumulated experience in adjusting the ideal calculations to its practice. Mathematized nature always remains beyond the direct grasp of praxis.

Equipped with this distinction between the ideal and material points of view, Galileo was far from blind to the leap beyond actual experience required by his mathematizing idealization. Yet once having made that leap, having conceived the physical universe in its parts and motions to be as precise and as rigorously determined as are the constructed idealities of geometry, indeed governed by the same mathematical relations, he had obtained the uniformity premise that would enable inductive reasoning to advance beyond the reach of finite experience. As a result of this aspect of his conception, he could say of those sciences in which mathematical demonstrations are applied to natural phenomena: "the principles, once established by well-chosen experiments, become the foundations of the entire superstructure."[32]

On the basis of this foundation, understanding could extend beyond those limited experiments with which it begins; it could reach beyond finite experience because

> The knowledge of a single fact acquired through a discovery of its causes prepares the mind to understand and ascertain other facts without need of recourse to experiment.[33]

The "causes" referred to here are neither the final causes so dear to the Peripatetics nor even efficient causes; they are geometrical "causes." And these, understood through "the force of rigid demonstrations such as occur only in mathematics,"[34] contain the possibility for infinite extension owing to the character of mathematics itself as an ideal technique, although one that was not fully developed in its formal aspects until long after Galileo's day.

These essential aspects of Galileo's concept, according to which the world is isolated from human will, ordered by universal principles, and revealed ideally to mathematical thought, constitute the basic presupposition of what "Galilean science" set out to comprehend. These aspects define the domain that must be understood in advance of experiment and mathematical demonstrations, for such "proofs" yield necessary and universal "physical conclusions" only with respect to a domain so characterized. In this way, the structure of Galileo's underlying conception established the norms of a shared meaning horizon within which mathematical formulae may be understood to express the Laws of Nature.

And yet, the aim of natural science as a project, itself determined by this prescientific conception, could not then become a theme for investigation within science. Nor could the concept be verified in its fundamental aspects by subsequent scientific inquiry. Such verification could only be approached through an infinite, and therefore ideal, process. It was this fact Husserl indicated as the *crisis* in modern European sciences.[35] Although Galilean science could do nothing within its own methodology but take this underlying concept for granted, when we come to see the concept itself as the result of an originary expression, as the characterization of a meaning horizon established in an act of creative expression, then scientific conclusions in turn are seen to be based upon an act of interpretation directed in the first instance toward our own surrounding world.

But when scientific conclusions are taken as strictly objective, and as the discovery of facts that themselves are held to be independent of any meaning horizon, then scientific discourse itself has been deflected from its own genuine foundations and has been allowed to slip into the practice of idle talk. It has become the passing along of available meanings, without any current revitalization and reclaiming of the primary experiences and their inventive expressions that set forth the meaning horizon in which those meanings are grounded.

The assimilation of creativity to discovery in science is indicative of the view Husserl called "physicalistic objectivism,"[36] according to which the world is objectively pregiven to every rational being and *in itself* unconditionally valid for all. As concerned with a world that is presupposed, this view is said to move away from and forget its own origins. Since it has done so, it has tended to treat the products of creative expression as the objective results of ingenious or felicitous discoveries, that is, as "objective" knowledge fixed by and then inherited from the tradition.

Once physicalistic objectivism has been inherited as a prevailing epistemology, if not perhaps an epistemological ideology, objective facts immediately come loose from their origins and are then available to be passed along, to be refined in detail and supplemented with others, as needed, to ensure scientific "completeness." As a result of this view, as well as the technical character of both experiment and mathematical explanation, the information accumulated within the institution of science can be passed along and remain effective within certain limits, even though the required correspondences, which give these techniques their sense as means for knowing the world, remain entirely implicit because lodged in the structure of the meaning horizon and are never again brought to awareness as a problem.

Inheriting its meaning horizon from the past through the adoption of the Galilean concept and interpreting the origin of that concept as a discovery, science itself has become a thought separated from its expression, *gedacht* while no longer *gedichtet*. This severance follows from the forgetfulness of the creative origin, and from the failure to do what is required to make any concept genuinely one's own: to reconstitute its meaning on the vital ground of one's own world as experienced, to reenact the creative act this time as the structuring of one's own world.

According to Nietzsche, even interpretation of a concept or formula must be creative.[37] But scientific objectivism precludes such a response to the concept of "world." At bottom, this is a meaning that has been passed along, and it is passed around—implicitly in everyday dealings, and more directly, although still implicitly for the most part, in formal scientific training and work. Taken for granted as obvious both in workaday scientific activity and in the derived "natural attitude," this concept inevitably appears to have "originated" in a discovery, not in an act of creative expression. Accordingly, it is taken over from others, and the need for its vital recreation is covered over; indeed the very possibility of any recreative thought is a fortiori denied along with any originary expression that may still pass as initially creative. As a result, the vital role of creativity in the origin and continuing life of the scientific tradition, as well as in the generally shared meaning horizon, is thoroughly overlooked.

Jointly, the aspects I have maintained to be essential to Galileo's underlying concept constituted an objectification and idealization of physical nature and expressed the idea of a methodically and univocally determinable world, already established in itself and universally valid for every rational being. On the basis of this accomplishment, itself unexamined and indeed unexaminable by scientific methods, Galilean science sought to carry out its project. Because of its rapid and evident progress, its techniques gained the reputation as the epitome of rational inquiry. Thus, it was either overlooked or held to be harmless that the concept underlying mathematical physics, and in turn the whole of modern natural science, is the idea of a world that is only thinkable, and hardly accessible, even indirectly, to experience.

Galileo himself remained cognizant of the leap required to interpret idealized mathematical entities as representing experienced physical nature, but through the forgetfulness that accompanies specialization, encouraged by the character of mathematicophysical science as technique, this conceptual leap came to be taken for granted. Galileo's historical influence rests not so much on his having made this leap, for we all make it, more or less cognizantly, as on his having made it so persuasively that it could be passed on as a matter of course and no longer appear in need of interrogation. Because of this unquestioning acceptance and the universal-mathematical character of the concept, his achievement also prepared the way for the development, in a newly compelling manner, of the concept of an ideal world ultimately accessible only through the methods and formulae of mathematical thought.

Drawing on the faith in mathematical reasoning[38] as comprehending the "truth" of *ta onta,* Galileo reawakened Plato's project. By conceiving physical nature as that which truly and absolutely is and as such corresponds to the necessary demonstrations of mathematical reasoning, he offered a means of ascending out of the shadowy cave of *doxa: epistémé* was to be reached through a dialectic now realized as *mathesis*.

Yet, as with Plato's *eidos,* the Galilean world proved to be beyond the reach of human experience, separated now by the idealization inherent in the construction of mathematical entities—a separation revealed by the leap required to interpret these entities as representing experienced physical nature.

To the modern interpreter Galileo will be seen as having planted in the conception underlying modern natural science the seeds of a Platonism whose fruits would not be fully recognized as such until they ripened into science's own crisis in the twentieth century, when its loss of meaning for human life motivated a few philosophers, preeminently Husserl, to examine radically its foundation. In essence, when creativity in science is treated as technical discovery, that institution betrays its own origins and exhibits an impoverished self-understanding that shows up in the crisis such patterns of thought must eventually undergo. Where Galileo had been long revered as the founder of modern science, his creative contribution to the development of the scientific institution becomes transvalued in Husserl's investigation into the crisis of the modern European sciences. And when a creative scientific act runs itself out, only another—in this historical instance, one in philosophy itself—will add further impetus to the living institution.

We may move in this way from Galilean science to Husserlian phenomenology.

CHAPTER 3

Husserl and the Life-World

On the preceding interpretation, Galileo's creative expression represented a threefold achievement: it codified the concept of an objective, though idealized, physical universe as the theme for natural science; it instituted experimental methods as the proper mode of access to that subject matter; and it established mathematical language as the medium for explanation. By thus determining what was to be investigated, how the inquiry was to be conducted, and the means whereby the results were to be expressed, he set up what I have called a "meaning horizon" whose structure exhibited the norms for a self-contained program of infinite tasks. On the basis of this achievement and within the context it established, exact physical sciences were instituted and made impressive systematic advances, both in the direction of *theoria* and toward ever greater technical control over the experienced physical environment.

And yet, despite the evident progress along these two lines, the underlying relation between them remained unclarified. The relation between the concept of an ideal, mathematized, objective nature and the experienced world of constantly changing phenomena rested on nothing more secure than Galileo's "book of Nature" metaphor—a reminder, perhaps, of Nietzsche's dictum that for anything to be *gedacht* it must first be *gedichtet*. The practical and theoretical successes in the sciences, however, beginning immediately with Galileo, tended to make this relation itself appear to be objective fact, even though one that could not be verified by the methods that depended upon it. Those successes gave to Galileo's metaphor the appearance of an adequate expression of the basis for an experimental and mathematical inquiry into the natural world. In turn, they buttressed the view that the objective world so comprehended comprises the universe of all that is, indeed the universal "meaning horizon."

Given this outlook, it is easy to see how the methods of mathematical physics could take on the status of a paradigm for all understanding whatsoever, even though this role pressed these methods beyond their proper function legitimated by the Galilean conception. It is clear on reflection that Galilean science is restricted to a carefully limited domain—objective physical nature in its quantifiable properties. And on its own principles that science can do no better than presuppose such a nature and merely assert its ideal character whereby it is related to mathematical language.

Nevertheless, the weight of scientific progress had far-reaching effects, and perhaps most profoundly on the philosophical community. In Descartes, Galileo's younger contemporary, we already find the idea of a "universal mathematics" shaping the methods of reasoning. The effects are also to be found in those philosophers of the Enlightenment, such as Locke, Hume, and Kant, who saw a need to examine more critically the conceptual foundations of this new and powerful approach to interpreting nature. The result, as Edmund Husserl described it three centuries later, was nothing less than a transformation of the concept of the world, and in turn, of philosophy:

> Thus the world and, correlatively, philosophy, take on a completely new appearance. The world must, in itself, be a rational world, in the new sense of rationality taken from mathematics, or mathematized nature; correspondingly, philosophy, the universal science of the world, must be built up as a unified rational theory *more geometrico*.[1]

Significantly, this response by the philosophers illustrates precisely how the inventive character of Galileo's achievement becomes obscured. When the correlation between mathematical ideality and experienced nature is taken to be objectively valid, Galileo's assertion of the correspondence appears not to be a creative expression, inventively establishing—in Husserl's term, "constituting"—a new "meaning horizon"; rather it appears merely to express the discovery of an important "fact" about nature.

Whatever historical importance may have been accorded Galileo's achievement, the tendency to treat it as a discovery indicates that the meaning horizon announced by his metaphor is already operative. But it is precisely this doctrine of "physicalistic objectivism," or as Husserl also calls it "naive objectivism," that must be suspended and put into question, according to his program, in order to gain a secured and clarified foundation for the natural sciences. For this purpose, Husserl maintained, nothing short of a "genuinely radical inquiry"—an inquiry that would first suspend the objectivism of the physical sciences, and indeed of the modern "natural attitude," so that the relation between any idea for a workaday scientific program and the intuitively experienced world might be clarified—would serve. The exigency of this task was brought to bear on Husserl by what he perceived to be the twentieth-century crisis of the sciences and of Western culture generally.

For one thing, the impending self-destruction of European society, which was already evident during the portentous lull between the two world wars, made clear to an unprecedented degree the urgent necessity for gaining a basis for establishing norms that would direct the use of natural science and its technology toward the benefit of "human" concerns. It was this technology that had so greatly intensified the threat of catastrophe by giving enormous powers of destruction to nations at war. At the same time, the overwhelming acceptance of objective-scientific principles effectively eliminated any other norms for rationally directing the life of society. If the societal conditions required for the continuation of scientific inquiry were to be maintained, then the culture that nurtured the scientific institution must be preserved. More importantly, the scientific institution itself had to be redirected toward the fulfillment of values more deeply rooted in the "human spirit" than those of strictly objective inquiry.

In response to the rather "pragmatic" nature of this crisis, Husserl saw that natural scientific methods and principles were inadequate for directing a defense against the threat of society's imminent demise, and this inadequacy in turn revealed that the view of physicalistic objectivism, which determined science's domain, was itself inadequate as a framework within which to establish new norms capable of resolving the critical situation. For the same reasons, he perceived that social psychology could not be expected to provide adequate solutions, because of its aspirations for becoming a natural science itself.

Motivated, perhaps, by this crisis in the "life-world," Husserl recognized that a solution had to be sought there also. It was clear that strictly within the Galilean program the only consistent aim is to understand and control physical nature. In this regard the objectivism basic to that task could not be faulted for providing no standards that would be relevant outside its proper context, either for guiding the practical application of technology or for directing other social institutions. It was, after all, precisely by abdicating such responsibility and rights that the independence of scientific inquiry had been acquired. But when this abdication came to be expected of all rational thought and resulted in the refusal to accept the barest possibility of any other kind of norm, especially in the face of the imminent breakdown of the entire society, it represented a denial of the social and cultural concerns characteristic of the Renaissance culture that gave birth to Galilean science and that gave it meaning for human life.

Although Galileo argued strenuously for the independence of scientific methods, even to the detriment of his own well-being before the tribunals of the Church, it is clear that for him and the wisest of his contemporaries such independence was relative and remained strictly within a broader meaning horizon in which the purpose and value of scientific inquiry could be seen to lie in its contribution to the welfare of people and societies. Galileo's difficulty was to be caught between two incompatible intellectual allegiances, wherein the party with the weaker claims disposed of the greater institutional power. To escape the difficulty would require the existence of two conditions, necessarily lacking at the birth of the new meaning horizon: (i) the well-grounded state of scientific inquiry and (ii) the general recognition of the institutional nature of science itself.

If natural science had become firmly established as a powerful institution by the early twentieth century, its independence had been interpreted in an extreme manner that was alien to its Renaissance origins, and this interpretation made the issue of its grounding all the more difficult. The self-enclosed and objective character of science's subject matter and the self-sufficiency of its methods had come to be taken as indicating a closed and entirely self-contained meaning horizon—one that was freed absolutely from subjective and "human" concerns. These in turn were relegated to the intuitive and inexact *Geisteswissenschaften.*

But these "humanistic disciplines"[2] lacked the stolid methods and fixed concepts needed to chart the systematic progress that might have allowed them to be viewed as co-equal with the *Naturwissenschaften*. Neither could they gain an independent subject matter, in a manner analogous to that of the latter, by abstracting from all physical nature so as to obtain a self-enclosed domain of pure psychic activity. The view that the human spirit is grounded on corporeity, first of single individuals and then of these in an interaction whereby a community is formed, seemed to make the human sciences inevitably dependent upon the physical sciences: an exact and thorough explanation within the former would have to be carried out ultimately on the basis of physics and chemistry.

In the factual absence of the psychophysiological account that might establish this connection, all talk about deriving norms from the humanistic disciplines that might direct scientific and other social institutions would remain "soft," as a result of the "subjective" origins of those disciplines and their presumed inability to satisfy any criteria for establishing the validity of meanings. On the other hand, even if the complex research difficulties that deferred the realization of such an account were overcome, its roots in the *Naturwissenschaften* would predetermine that it could only confirm the dependent status of the human sciences. The values treated therein would necessarily have been reduced to "objective" facts concerning the psychic activity of valuing; they could not then take precedence over the norms inherent in the fundamental conception on which their investigation was based. The view of the "hard" sciences as self-contained would remain unshaken and continue to deny any possibility of norms for directing the objective sciences that were not strictly their own, namely furthering *theoria* and increasing technical control over physical nature. With or without the psychophysiological account, these sciences collectively would continue to be interpreted as absolutely independent. And the grounding for such inquiries in a broader meaning horizon would remain problematic, if recognized as needed at all.

Yet if the natural sciences in their modern state were still constitutionally incapable of responding to the threat of destruction facing the society that nurtured them, it was clear to Husserl that any philosophy founded on the same physicalistic objectivism would likewise be inadequate to the task. To the extent that the philosophical institution had adopted "naturalism" as its conceptual context and had accepted as absolute the scientific criteria for establishing the validity of meanings, its only proper tasks would be seen to lie in the service of natural science, now, after the early successes of the Galilean program, a recognized institution in its own right. Philosophy's own norms, then, would exhibit the same limitations in relation to the contemporaneous crisis as those of the exact mathematical sciences. It too needed a new foundation.

When Husserl diagnosed the sickness of European humanity in his Vienna Lecture of 1935,[3] he saw himself as taking on the difficult task of awakening the philosophical community to its responsibility as "the functionaries of mankind."[4] In his elucidation of the (by then familiar) theme of the European crisis, he sought to recall philosophy and its "branches," the natural sciences, to their historical-teleological obligations arising out of their own origins in the unique culture he called "spiritual Europe."[5] By this he meant the culture that had been given birth in Greece in the seventh and sixth centuries B.C. by the irruption of the concept of mankind's freely shaping its existence through ideas of reason. Commitment to this concept characterized the vocational activity to which the Greeks had given the name *philosophia.* And the epoch of history initiated by this invention represented to Husserl a cultural tradition in which mankind had been set on a path toward its highest possible fulfillment. The danger of an abrupt halt to this epoch brought about by a "misguided rationalism"[6] motivated his call to an understanding of the origins of philosophy itself.

In order to fulfill the essential functions projected in its historical origins, philosophy was called upon to reverse the relation between itself and the physical sciences that had developed during the previous three centuries. Instead of continuing as handmaiden to the sciences, philosophy was challenged to reassert its earlier status as "universal science," as genuine "first philosophy." In order to regain this status rightfully, however, the modern institution of philosophy would have to disentangle itself from the naive objectivism and naturalism that, according to Husserl, had diverted reason into overly specialized areas of methodical but limited inquiry. The crisis demanded that philosophy seek new foundations, for itself as well as for the dependent "regional" sciences. And these foundations, when brought to a new "scientific" clarity, would reveal mankind's own role in constituting the objective-natural meaning horizon within which the physical sciences operated so effectively. When this conceptual context was seen to be humanly and historically established, and grounded in a prior understanding of the horizon of significance Husserl termed the "life-world," the institution of science could be held accountable to "ideas of reason" that were not themselves confined to objective-mathematical criteria for establishing the validity of meanings. Social and cultural values, "spiritual" values, although inoperative in strictly scientific (that is, objective) inquiry, could be reasserted by the renewed "first philosophy" as legitimate norms for the project of shaping man's existence. The mathematical-physical sciences, then, rather than dominating that project, would be powerful tools in its service.

This call to an inquiry into foundations did not, however, imply a return to the "metaphysical" procedures practiced by Aristotelians. Galileo's overthrow of those methods had been too successful to be disdained. His emphasis on experience, basic to experimental methods, had too thoroughly proved itself to be rejected out of hand. The new foundations would have to be based in experience, and indeed in the troublesome subjective experience of the intuited world in which phenomena are ever changing and where mathematically exact determinations can only be approached as ideal limits. Even Galileo's method begins with such experience, but his hasty leap to geometrical analysis, and to the ideal nature it presupposes, leaves the crucial correspondence between geometry and nature unclarified.

Husserl's insight, which if successfully carried out would allow his program to avoid the misguided rationalism at the root of the crisis in the European sciences between the two world wars, was to see that this correspondence could be secured if the concepts of geometry and nature themselves could be grounded in the subjective, but nevertheless real and eidetically constant, experience of the philosopher or scientist who would understand the world via their use. For this reason the methodological techniques he had developed earlier—*epoché*, reduction, and constitution—were revised in light of the newer concept of the "life-world."

In its earlier applications, for instance, in *Ideas* and *Cartesian Meditations*,[7] *epoché* had functioned as the suspension in a single step of all validities posited by the thinking ego, so that corporeal nature as well as societal and cultural formations and all other egos were at once reduced to phenomena. Although these still appeared in their full typical significance, the reflecting ego withheld commitment to their thetic sense as indicating self-subsistent being; that is, the validity of their independent, objective existence was held in suspense, prevented from being operative in the analysis of their meanings. In this way the *epoché* was said to lead immediately to the pure transcendental ego, and from this "absolute" base phenomenological *constitution* was to commence.

But in his last words on phenomenology, *The Crisis of European Sciences and Transcendental Phenomenology*,[8] a newly emphasized historical concern, focused upon "the origins of our critical scientific and philosophical situation," was combined with a new application of his techniques. The procedure of *epoché* was articulated into a series of suspensions. The first step now places in "brackets" the validity only of the objective sciences, leaving intact commitment to the life-world as it is revealed to a prescientific attitude, where the "typical style" of the natural world is held in "doxic certainty." Whereas in the further steps Husserl again goes after the transcendental ego, it is through this initial reduction of scientific nature, and the account of its constitution as a meaning structure that is accomplished through "intentional analysis," that he aims to reveal new foundations for objective science.

When the validity of the natural sciences is held in abeyance, and their acquired facts and theoretical constructs are "put out of play," clearly we do not find ourselves in the utter confusion that would result from a totally unstructured world. Instead, in this methodically acquired prescientific attitude, we find that a certain order is still evident, communication remains possible, and hence a shared horizon of significance remains in effect. Husserl refers to this prescientific horizon as the "life-world" (*die Lebenswelt*). This implicit horizon, which emerges when the scientific framework is "bracketed," is described as the constantly presupposed horizon for all cultural achievements, the context within which all meaning structures, including the natural sciences, have been erected.

Although attention is ordinarily dominated by particular, specialized interest horizons, for example, one's vocational "world," so that one takes into account only those aspects of the full life-world that are relevant to the work at hand, it becomes clear on reflection that any possible effective life, or any possible vocational activity, including that of the natural scientist, takes place within this general horizon. With this concept, then, Husserl calls to our attention the commonly shared context wherein objective science has arisen as a significant tradition, initially instituted by Galileo's achievement and then further developed by a vocational community committed to the resulting methods and norms. The scientific vocation and the sedimented meanings peculiar to its tradition are thus brought back into contact with mankind's other activities and concerns, even while the unique features proper to it are preserved.

One such feature of objective science as a meaning structure is its systematic character; each new acquisition depends upon what has come before and has for its "premises" all scientific acquisitions. This means that the earlier achievements can always be reconfirmed, precisely by reactivating the procedures whereby they were first obtained. This requirement holds on principle, even if an explicit reactivation of the entire chain of evidence comes to be impractical in the later stages of its development. Eventually this chain leads back to an appeal to "what stands there" as self-evident to prescientific experience, either strictly within an experimental context or merely in an observation of the unmanipulated natural world. In thus appealing to the evidence of "ordinary" experience, objective science itself is brought to acknowledge the life-world as its own presupposition, as it must do if it is to represent a means of comprehending the world that we live in, to any degree.

This purpose remained clear to Galileo. But in Husserl's view, the practice of modern science had revealed a loss of commitment to this aim of being meaningful for human life. Even though physical science's ultimate evidence still lay in the life-world (for this includes the indicator devices of the most sophisticated laboratory equipment), the concept of this region had come to be considered unacceptable, that is, nonscientific, through the rise of objective-mathematical criteria as the only means for establishing the validity of meanings. On these criteria the only valid concept of a universal horizon must be constructed through a method of summation over the ideal totality of particular objects. By this mode of thinking the attention of modern science had been diverted to a substrate accessible only through technology and theory. As a result, not only had the connection of scientific inquiry with the life-world, obvious in Galileo's day, become obscure, but its explicit retention had been dismissed as bootless. By granting ontic status exclusively to this now thoroughly mathematized substrate, modern science had lost its meaning for human life. The poverty of the "misguided rationalism" Husserl saw as characteristic of the technological-scientific age was brought into even clearer focus when this reversal of priority also infected the social sciences and psychology, as a result of their emulation of objective-mathematical criteria.

In order to effect a counterreversal, and to show how modern science might be brought back into proper relation to the disparaged "subjective" norms, Husserl sought to exhibit science's own grounding in the life-world. The challenge was to provide an account of the transition from this prescientific region to the ideal objective substrate intended by scientific thought. Galileo had made the leap to this ideal construct with his assumption of geometry's superior capability, in relation to common intuition, as a means for understanding experienced nature; thus he could claim for physical science a suprahistorical validity that previously had been reserved to the purely ideal sciences, such as pure mathematics and pure geometry itself. But when Husserl suspended the validity of Galileo's mathematization of nature he saw that the transition itself, that is, the move to an ideal conceptual model, was necessarily historical; it was a constitutive act, not only with respect to physical science but also with respect to its original conceptual tool, geometry.

Both pure and applied geometry, then, had to be accounted for as the result of a historical process that began in a meaning horizon that would initially lack what was to be attained only upon the successful realization of the process. Geometry, too, had to have been constituted as a meaning structure. The idealization through which exact geometrical shapes and ideal space are conceived was described by Husserl as a constructive procedure beginning with the merely approximate but habitually typical constancies of the surrounding world given to ordinary experience.[9] It is easy to see how this process must have emerged, first as a possibility, then as a valued accomplishment, initially motivated by needs arising from social *praxis*: to distribute goods equally, to survey the land, to acquire consistently shaped building blocks. In short, the need for concepts of perfection, Husserl maintained, is generated by life-world needs, and the standards of precision are at first set quite practically.

Practical precision, however, admits of degrees: specifically, it can be increased, for example, by observing more closely, or, in the case of magnitude, by employing a standard designed so as to mark off multiples of itself; and the techniques for measuring can themselves be made more and more precise. In regard to shape, the particular province of geometry, certain regular figures among the many perceived will stand out as most "significant," that is, as most practical for a particular use. Straight edges and circles, cylinders and cubes, for example, will emerge as they prove more functional than less regular shapes, although merely in an approximation appropriate to their intended purpose. Two building blocks that are to meet tightly will be carefully chiseled then polished smooth in a process directed toward achieving flat surfaces. Practical limitations and the needs of the job will determine at first what counts as flat. But the process itself aims for, and thereby "defines," the surface that would be achieved if all irregularities were removed by repeating the process again and again: an exactly flat surface. In this way the notion of the ideal shape arises in the life-world as the anticipation of what would be obtained if the practical limitations were removed and the process carried on in its same direction, but with an endless continuation that can be conceived of as possible. Thus, the ideal shape is said to result from a privation of the perceived shape: the "perfectly flat" surface is the observed surface lacking its imperfections.

Merely observing the progressive approach, in an actual development, toward a complete lack of imperfection, however, suggests an idea that cannot be thought determinately until it is also possible to think the infinitely reiterated "again and again" as having been run through. To establish firmly the indicated concept, a constructive method of thought is required, and moreover one that is equipped with the idea of an iteration that can be freely renewed with unconditional and self-evidently possible infinity. This methodological idea of infinite iteration is also an accomplishment, Husserl maintains, and it occurs not in the realm of "pure intuition" but rather in that of practical concerns directed toward the experienced world. It is here that the conception of an endless continuation in the direction of the prior design of the series first arises. As gradual, this continuation offers a basis, in the life-world, for a conception of the infinity of imperfection, and the process of removing imperfections, gradually but iterated to infinity, motivates the idea of perfection.[10] When the series is pressed ever further with the aid of improved techniques, and the possibility of its perfect fulfillment is conceived, that is, when its ideal end is projected, limit-shapes emerge as thinkable though never practically attainable poles.

Real *praxis* concerned with empirical possibilities is thereby supplemented with an ideal *praxis* concerned solely with the realm of perfect limit-shapes. Having abstracted from empirical restrictions, it is possible for the empty design of a merely endless series to be filled in by the constructed idea of the aim toward which an infinite series tends. The shapes, which stand out first in a merely approximate fashion, can then be perfectly determined, univocally and in advance, according to universal operations. With the development and systematization of these operations, there emerges the actually attainable possibility of constructing determinately, though only in "thought," all possibly conceivable ideal shapes. This is the method, codified by Euclid and already secure in tradition, that Galileo inherited as the science of "pure geometry."

A further step, however, is needed to complete the transition from the life-world to Galilean nature. A process of objectification is required in order to bring the perceived object into harmony with the exactly determined concepts of geometry. This too is a matter of method founded upon prescientific experience. Husserl attributes the pre-Galilean phase of this development to a mutually enhancing interchange between the ideal *techné* of pure geometry and the practical art of measuring and surveying—an interchange that suggested an ideally determinate object underlying the observed object, always revealed with only relative precision.

Knowledge of things in the obviously existing empirical world, Husserl notes, "remains unwaveringly approximate, suspended in vague differentiations of greater or less perfection."[11] But the fact that more precise determination may be gained through moving the thing closer implies an open horizon of always possibly greater precision. Moreover, each thing so encountered implies another open horizon: that of further experiences of other things. And this horizon extends in possibility to the ideal totality of things that make up the physical stratum of the life-world. Through communalization of experiential life the "normal certainty" arises that each of us encounters the same objects that others do, and that all objects actually or possibly encountered by others can likewise be encountered by each of us. This certainty applies to the entire life-world as the horizon for all possible human experience. Out of one's own ongoing harmonious experience, and its consistency with reports available in communal life, a habitual style that characterizes the experienced world, a style consisting of typical constancies and general repetitions, emerges.

On closer examination, however, the experience of the life-world and the knowledge it gives rise to remain relative to those who experience. Neither ideally exact knowledge, nor knowledge of universal necessity is yet attained here. Knowledge of the life-world is characterized, in Husserl's phrase, by "doxic certainty." Even so qualified, this is the immediate basis, he maintained, for genuine *epistémé*.

In a further step—again constitutive of new meanings—universal and objective scientific knowledge is attained, but only through the accomplishments of methods by which doxic certainty in its turn is "perfected." A constructive process of objectification effects this move to the idea of an exactly determined object, and to the idea of an exact universal causality, that is, to the idea of a rationally knowable *in-itself* that, however, exhibits itself only relatively and subjectively. Like the idealization resulting in geometry's domain, this process too must begin in a meaning horizon initially lacking what is achieved only through its successful execution. Indeed, Husserl's analysis of the origin of geometry is exemplary here, even as geometry itself was exemplary for the historical objectification of scientific nature.

Husserl's account of the origin of geometry had shown how the idea of an exactly determined object is reached by considering it merely with regard to its shape, and then by thinking the approximating process of an infinite "again and again" as having been run through, so that the result of the process may be determined ideally and in advance through a method of construction. The shape-properties had thereby been idealized, and this provided an example for thought of "a thing as such in unconditional generality."[12] The method of reaching this idea, already established in geometry, set the pattern for constructing the concept of a "true" object constituted by the totality of its pure properties. When defined as the object in-itself, this ideal totality functions as the principle of unity underlying the series of actual and possible harmonious experiences of that object, even though the properties are exhibited only in relatively exact appearances, and in a merely finite portion of the infinite series of possible appearances.

In the same way, geometry had provided a model for objectifying and universalizing the intuitive causal style of the life-world. By its construction of ideal space as encompassing all conceivable shapes and by its formulation of the a priori rules that govern transformations within that space, geometry had demonstrated the systematic methods that, when applied to the objects of all possible world-experience *idealiter*, would result in the constructed concept of an ideal, universally ordered, and self-subsistent physical universe as the "field" containing all objects. The conceived continuation toward infinite perfection of possible external experience, and toward the ideal totality of its objects, accomplished through method, would conquer the finitude of actual experience and determine the idealized world as "an ideal infinity of things, each of which is itself an index for an ideal infinity of relative exhibitings whose harmonious unit of identity—*idealiter*—the thing is."[13]

The obvious, though subjective-relative causal style and spatiotemporal character of the life-world are then perfected and objectified through constructive methods analogous to those familiar in geometry. The result is an a priori idea of universal causal laws governing all changes within an ideal, objective space-time matrix as the "field" wherein any actual object must have its locus that will be determinable by indexicals.

Exact objectivity, best represented by modern classical physics, is thus accounted for by Husserl as the result of two accomplishments of method: first, a determined idealization of purely mathematical entities and then a "systematic operative construction of ideal objects out of pregiven objects."[14] These accomplishments imply particular ontic regions, each with its own proper mode of access to its constituent "elements." At the same time, the methods of construction enable their regions to be grasped "universally," and this provides the major premise for deductions and the "uniformity premise" for inductions with regard to the laws and events within that region.

In this way, Husserl accounts for the grounding of modern science in the life-world, as a meaning structure erected within history and owing its sense ultimately to prescientific experience and the "subjective" concerns familiar there. As grounded in the life-world, modern science cannot entirely dismiss either this region or the "doxic certainty" characteristic of our knowledge of it, however little these are needed in workaday scientific inquiry once its own methods and norms have been made available through the establishment of the particular meaning horizon for a scientific tradition.

In order for the meaning structures that make up modern science to regain their significance for human life, those structures must be understood, according to Husserl, in terms of the activity in which they are constituted, for example, those accomplishments described previously that are ultimately rooted in the life-world and that secure the possibility for an eventual, interpretive return to personal experience. In light of this focus on constitutive activity, Husserl saw that the claims to unconditional objective validity, made first on behalf of the purely a priori sciences and then devolving onto the rational sciences of fact as a result of their use of the former as methods, could be understood, and indeed justified in relation to their proper domain, only through an elucidation of the psychic activity whereby these sciences themselves had come to be established. This activity, Husserl emphasized, is "an accomplishment of human beings who find themselves in the world, the world of general experience."[15] And precisely because it is psychic activity, it must remain hidden to objective physical science, even though it is the "essence" of that undertaking as an activity of seeking and acquiring meanings. Objective science is peculiar, Husserl notes, because the meaning activity of the scientist must always remain invisible to it.[16]

Locke's general idea of a psychological-epistemological

approach to the modern enigmas of rational knowledge is therefore found to be entirely proper, even though his execution failed. It failed not merely because of his superficiality and unmethodical confusion, but more importantly because of the naturalism contained in his own psychology—the presupposition that opened the way for Hume's charges of fictionalism. Despite Hume's criticisms, which after all were themselves psychological, the psychological-epistemological approach should not be abandoned altogether in the manner of Kant's transcendental deduction, according to Husserl, because this gets us "involved in something incomprehensibly mythical."[17] Kant's transcendental faculties, which were intended to account for the requisite accomplishments, are by his own report not capable of being experienced. Husserl calls them "mythical constructions," because "we are in principle unable to make [them] intuitive to ourselves, whether through factual examples or through genuine analogy."[18] Rather than seeking an "intuitively disclosing method, intuitive in its point of departure and in everything it discloses," Kant was content with a "constructively inferring method," that is, his transcendental deduction of the conditions necessary for the possibility of experience.[19]

On the other hand, Husserl does find a valuable insight in Kant's transcendental philosophy, namely, its recognition that the functions that give the form to experience, that actively constitute meanings, and that procure validity for the theoretical constructs of objective knowledge necessarily lie in a dimension that is inaccessible to natural, objective experience and hence is also inaccessible to the objective sciences. Nevertheless, Husserl maintains, even as transcendental these functions do not belong to an anonymous "I" behind all experience, as Kant would have it. Rather they belong to a dimension of the "living spirit." As such these functions can be made accessible to experience, though of a peculiar sort to be sure, and only by a new method that itself requires a fundamental "change of attitude." What is more, this type of experience, which is not "Kantian scientific experience" and which does not have objective certainty (in the sense found in physics), can be exhibited with truly apodictic certainty as the experiential ground for all meaning producing activity, including that of objective scientific inquiry. It can, Husserl promises, be made accessible "through a method of disclosure appropriate to its realm of experiential and theoretical self-evidence."[20] Thus a genuinely "scientific" understanding, though of a new sort, is projected.

Husserl's own creative accomplishment, I am contending, was the codification of this new science's theme and the development of its methods, which will be directed to disclosing the eidetic, "transcendental" structures of subjective experience. Within the context thus established, he was able to account for the origins and validity of meanings through the notion of a fundamental subjective act of sense bestowal (*Sinngebung*).

In his final effort to introduce transcendental phenomenology, that is, in the *Crisis,* he first illustrated the method in regard to the objective sciences and thereby clarified the important modern opposition between physicalistic objectivism and the new outlook he characterized as transcendental subjectivism. "Bracketing" the validity of objective science revealed the ground of the life-world given to a prescientific natural attitude. From this ground, taken in its doxic certainty, he could describe the historical development of a meaning structure that had come to be taken as *epistémé* within the scientific and philosophical traditions. This description uncovered the creative conceptions, effective in the construction of an ideal, objective domain, that allowed for the transition from "natural philosophy" to "natural science."

The teleological-historical reflection on this transition, in Part II of the *Crisis,* may be seen as propaedeutic to the presentation of two ways into transcendental phenomenology that occupies the unfinished third part of that work. In Part III Husserl's techniques are applied first to the life-world and then to psychology, for the purpose of introducing these newly articulated ways into a genuine, apodictic, and self-substantiating science of transcendental subjectivity. When this science will have been established, the transition will have been made from "moral philosophy" to a secured, phenomenologically grounded "moral science," that is, to a genuine *Geisteswissenschaft.*

Husserl's procedure for achieving this latter goal begins with the "transcendental *epoché.*" By it the validity of the life-world as a meaning structure is itself placed in suspense. The objects that are straightforwardly given to the natural attitude, in whatever ontic modality they may have, are thus reduced to phenomena. A purely theoretic-descriptive interest is then taken in how those objects come to have their typical meanings as held with doxic certainty by the engaged ego. This is the task of accounting for the constitution of life-world meanings, and of nature as prescientifically understood. It is accomplished through "intentional analysis," so called because it focuses on the acts of consciousness by which any meaning, or any "object for consciousness," is intended and on those objects precisely as intended.

With the thematic attention of the investigator loosened from engagement in the "what" of the original, natural experience, the "how" or manner of appearing is brought to light in an act of reflection upon the first-level conscious act. But because this original act is and remains the investigator's own, it is fully and apodictically accessible in the reflective moment. As such it provides the self-evidence of direct experience and can therefore stand as an ultimate, self-substantiating "empirical" ground. The field of transcendental functions, which Kant had sought through transcendental deduction, is thereby brought to thematic attention as directly experienced through Husserl's procedure of transcendental reduction. And this dimension of the living spirit becomes the self-evident subject matter for the theoretical interest of intentional analysis.

It is understandable, perhaps, that Husserl's texts are

often quite programmatic and set out areas of inquiry that he could not thoroughly investigate himself. As the pioneer explorer in this newly defined science, attempting to mark off the complex regions systematically for careful phenomenological work, he blazed a tortuous trail. Indeed, he often recognized his own operative methods only through subsequent reflection on what he had already accomplished. This pattern, which can be traced in his published writings,[21] exhibits an inherent characteristic of phenomenological inquiry: an act is performed by one fully engaged in the work at hand; a second act—this one reflective—is required to make thematic what had been merely operative before. The reflective act brings to light for the first time what had been transparent, and necessarily so, in the first-level act. Husserl expressed this fact with a quotation taken from *Faust*: "In the beginning is the deed."[22] He could have done as well by quoting Nietzsche to the end that the *gedichtet* always precedes the *gedacht*.

As a beginning for a newer interpretation of Nietzsche's dictum, we may commence with a summary account of Husserl's "scientific" creativity. Faced with the crisis in his own vocational world, and indeed in the broader cultural community, he was motivated to reflect on the origin of the "misguided rationalism" he believed that crisis revealed. In an effort to counteract the diversion of modern rationalism into strictly objective-scientific thinking, and to establish an appreciation for the validity of meanings and norms grounded in "transcendental subjectivity," he applied his now modified techniques of epoché, reduction, and constitution to the tradition of modern natural science, focusing first on Galileo's "mathematization of nature."

Conjointly these techniques make up a general method for judging the sense of any intention: as a result of performing the epoché, the intended object of the "bracketed" thought is reduced to a phenomenon, whereupon its manner of appearing may be explicitly examined and its basis in actual experience exhibited; in effect, the act of constituting a meaning may be retraced. And when this method is applied within a "teleological-historical reflection," as it was in the *Crisis,* the result may be a retracing of the complex series of acts, distributed among the representatives of a diffuse institution, whereby a meaning structure such as the one called Galilean science had been erected and established as the prevailing horizon of significance for an entire cultural epoch.

When intentional analysis is applied to modern physical science, it becomes clear that the ultimately pertinent phenomena are those given in prescientific experience of nature within the horizon of the life-world. After all, it is the world we live in that science purports to explain, and science's meaning for human life lies ultimately in its contribution to our understanding of and informed response to the ways our environment operates. Yet, because observed objects and events experienced on the level of the life-world are presented in merely approximate, subjective-relative fashion, they cannot support the claims to mathematical exactness and to universal validity made for scientific laws and principles. Because those claims have been made, and have been accepted in principle, it is clear that scientific thinking intends "objects" and a "nature" that are characterized by the same mathematical exactitude and conceptual clarity that belong only to ideally constructed entities, such as those treated by pure geometry. As such, these "objects" and this "nature" are not perceivable; they are only conceivable.

Thus scientific thinking is directed in the first instance to a domain of methodically constructed, ideal conceptual models—what Husserl called "theoretical-logical substructions."[23] Only in the second instance, that is, indirectly, does it attend to perceptually experienced nature. The explanatory power of these abstract models in this regard rests on their merely posited status as "strict reality" that lies beneath the veil of the perceived world, and on the causal efficacy attributed to them. This theoretically constructed "nature" is, as Galileo's metaphor asserted, accessible only through the language of mathematics.

Precisely because this theory of a mathematized nature has met with such obvious successes in terms of predicting and controlling experienced physical nature, its effective connection with the life-world cannot be denied, as Husserl recognized. And yet, the interpretation of this substrate, as a "true" world in-itself that supports and explains the vague and average constancies of everyday experience, indeed that causes them, remains underdetermined. In Husserl's intentional analysis this decidedly metaphysical interpretation is rendered pointless; the effectiveness of mathematical-physical science may be accounted for by a description of the peculiar "constitution" responsible for its basic concepts, that is, a series of meaning-giving acts rooted in the life-world. If the book of Nature is written in the language of mathematics, this need not mean that nature's God is a mathematician, but perhaps merely that nature's scientists are.

The constitution of scientific concepts is peculiar, at least with respect to Husserl's earlier use of this notion, because in this case the process is an intersubjective one, and moreover one whose earliest phases are lost in the dim reaches of history. Nevertheless, because these concepts are mathematical and belong to a systematic meaning structure, their inherited sense may at any time be reestablished. This characteristic allows for a reconstruction of the means by which that sense must have been initially acquired. Husserl focused his account of scientific origins on the beginnings of geometry and "physics," seeing that Galileo's conjoining of these disciplines resulted in the establishment of the meaning horizon for mathematical physics, which he took as the paradigm of modern natural science.

Commencing in a necessarily prescientific and pregeometric attitude, the ordinary intuition of typical shapes in experienced space is "perfected" through constructive methods of thought. Universal operations are systematically employed so as to obtain an ideally determined and necessarily objective totality of all possible shapes and the homogeneous "field" in which they must subsist. When the so-called secondary qualities of objects are interpreted as being dependent upon the "primary" shape properties, as they were by Galileo, the move has already been made to a mathematically ideal physical "object." Thus physics gains an "object" that is univocally determinable in advance, exactly and methodically. The subsequent ideal summation over the totality of all possible "objects" results in a fully determinate, universal "Nature."

Because this construction begins with the life-world and indeed is initially motivated by life-world needs, the same general structures obvious here in an approximate fashion will be found also in the "Nature" intended by scientific thinking, although now "perfected." For this reason "Nature" will be a practically effective, even though ideal, model. Deductions and predictions made with respect to it will be borne out by life-world experience, but only after the requisite allowances are made for "insignificant" discrepancies. It is understandable that the inevitable inaccuracies would be attributed to the "accidental" differences between subjects and thus that the ideal model would come to be taken as the fixed standard, eventually as "strict reality," precisely because it is methodically constructed.

Husserl described this natural-scientific mathematization as a procedure whereby "we measure the life-world . . . for a well-fitting *garb of ideas*," but, he adds, when we overlook the constructive origins of this *Ideenkleid* we risk making an ideology of physicalistic objectivism because we "take for *true being* what is actually a *method.*"[24] Even so, the universal character of this method enables it to provide an ideal model, a "theoretical-logical substruction," that will itself be universally applicable, in the sense that any object or event conceivably exhibited in the life-world will have its physical stratum and may therefore be analyzed with respect to its quantifiable physical properties. Because the model lends itself to a "universal" grasp, claims may justifiably be made for a general causality and for uniformity as regards its governing laws.

Although it is clear that the science of geometry treats ideal shapes in an ideal space, something like Husserl's technique of *epoché-reduction* was required to make it equally clear that mathematical physics likewise treats of an ideal domain. As the method of a "science of meanings," this technique reveals that the only possible means for exhibiting scientifically intended "Nature" will be the mental performance of the universal operations by which it is constructed as an "object for consciousness." Even though this mental activity, and its resulting intentional "object," belong strictly to the individual subjects who perform the constructive operation, because the operation is universal and directed by a general method, the constituted "nature" is indeed objective. Whatever consequences follow from its properties or governing laws for the experiences of one subject will likewise follow for those of another. Thus if I can anticipate a future appearance of some object or event, then we can expect its fulfillment, given the proper allowance for subjective, "accidental" discrepancies. And these differences are precisely what rigid experimental methods are designed to exclude.

Husserl's method of "intentional analysis," then, may be seen as analogous to Nietzsche's perception of the relation between what may be thought and what has already been produced in an act of creative expression. On this analysis, even the most objective of the modern sciences, mathematical physics, illustrates the insight cryptically expressed by Nietzsche: whatever we have been able to think in abstraction from an originary act of expression must already have been created in such acts—the *gedacht* founded in and created by the *gedichtet,* concepts in and by inventive expressions.[25]

If Husserl's account of the inventive conception of scientific "Nature," reached through idealization and objectification, reverses the metaphysical interpretation that would have these processes discover a "true" world in-itself and exhibits instead their character as constructive methods constitutive of a new meaning horizon, historically instituted and ultimately grounded in the life-world, then he remains obligated to account for the prior constitution of this original horizon itself, in its capacity as an intersubjective meaning structure that is "universally" grasped in the natural attitude.

By the time he was writing the *Crisis,* Husserl had come to recognize that the total intentional accomplishment of this meaning horizon, that is, the life-world, with its many levels of *Sinngebung,* does not belong to an isolated subject, as his earlier analyses had implied. He now saw that the meaning-giving activity responsible for this communally constituted horizon of significance belongs to "the entire intersubjectivity which is brought together in the accomplishment."[26] It is an activity that operates on the level of social interaction, and most explicitly through rational discourse. Thus he spoke at the last of a historical and "intersubjective constitution" performed by "human beings who find themselves in the world of general experience." And he acknowledged that only by systematically clarifying this truly complex historical and intersubjective operation can "the world as it is for us become understandable as a meaning structure formed out of elementary intentionalities."[27]

Even so, Husserl's continued insistence on these elementary intentionalities, as the ultimate fundament that is to be synthesized, bound him to the notion of a genuinely isolated transcendental ego: "the purely subjective in its own self-enclosed pure context as intentionality."[28] Its activity, as disclosed by a transcendental epoché, remains responsible for the original formation of ontic meaning, and only afterward can the communal operation commence. Yet despite his promises to the contrary, this ultimately original bestower of sense never is directly exposed by a genuine "intuitively exhibiting method." This elusive creature continues to withdraw into hiding with each further reduction. Like the mysterious "hide-behind" of southern folklore that is said to follow children who walk alone in the forests, no matter how quickly one turns around, it still hides behind him. The transcendental ego is never more than "logically" implicated by the results of its synthesizing function. So it too remains a "mythical construct."

Correlatively, despite the valuable insight expressed by the concept of the "life-world," in Husserl's account its constitution relies on a projective synthesis of elementary intentionalities. Moreover, because these are always characterized as present—either currently present, remembered as having been present, or anticipated as yet to be present—they require an even deeper structure of temporal synthesis "into the unit of one time."[29] Thus even beneath the synthetic constitution of the life-world, there lies the self-synthesizing of the transcendental ego into a single temporality. And this, Husserl admits in an unusual understatement, "leads to difficult investigations"[30]—an acknowledgement, perhaps, of his need to reconsider the earlier analysis of "the inner consciousness of time."[31]

Even on his latest account, then, the constituted world remains an ideal totality, and it can be reached only by a mathematical method of summation over two infinities: (i) the possible appearances of a single object and (ii) the totality of all possible objects. Not only is the "object" understood to be the principle of unity governing any possible appearance of "it" to some present intuition—that is, the projective synthesis of all its possible "profiles" that would be given *idealiter* in an infinite series of harmonious presentations—but the "world" too is understood to be a principle of unity, now universalized and projected as the ideal synthesis of the totality of such "objects." "*Die Welt ist alles, was der Fall ist,*" as Ludwig Wittgenstein stated the matter in the opening pronouncement of his logicophilosophical treatise.[32] This "world," however, cannot be brought to exhibit itself unitarily as a phenomenon, in the manner required of the life-world if it is to be the original horizon implicit in any elementary intentionality.

What is more, on this account the "world" so constituted remains thoroughly ontic, that is, composed of particular entities. Therefore it cannot serve the required ontological function as the ultimate meaning horizon that is pregiven whenever any particular intention has the significance of an entity for its sense. In order for this horizon, which Husserl intended under the name of *life-world,* to be disclosed in its ontological character, an elucidation must be forthcoming of that being whose "life" exhibits the essential capacity for creatively establishing "worlds" of meaning: that being whose very existence determines "contexts of significance."

For these reasons the success of Husserl's creative accomplishment was restricted to the institution of a method, and indeed a "science," whereby the meanings already presupposed in the Galilean sciences received genuine elucidation for the first time. This contribution, moreover, set up the "philosophical" context that provided the basis, I shall contend, for the further creative development of phenomenological ontology, even though Husserl denigrated this effort under the pejorative title of *Existenzphilosophie.*

Like Galileo's, his own originary expression represents a threefold achievement: it establishes the psychic dimension of the living spirit as the theme for transcendental phenomenology; it develops "intentional analysis" as the descriptive method for the investigation; and it shows how "ordinary language" can serve as its expressive medium. As a result, a "science of meanings" is instituted: a science directed to analyzing the meanings with which we interpret the significance of the world we live in.

Whereas Galileo's science focused on what the world may be discovered to be, Husserl's focused on how the world is given to understanding. In a further creative advance within phenomenology itself, achieved by Heidegger, the focus will be on who understands the world and himself along with it. This inquiry, although retaining Husserl's reflective methods and still treating a "transcendental" dimension, will not seek a transcendental ego; nor will it rely solely on pure description of the structures of consciousness as revealed by an eidetic reduction. On the contrary, instead of "bracketing" all ontic validities, Heidegger will analyze precisely the existential structures of human being, interpreted as that being whose " 'essence' . . . lies in its existence." Because human beings necessarily reveal an existing world, this inquiry may begin with the inherited everyday understanding of the life-world. Its own creative contribution will be to disclose ontological understanding implicit in ontic understanding, even when the traditional expression of the former had been deflected by the latter, in a forgetfulness of man's unique status as the one who is given to understand his own being along with that of his world.

This turn of phenomenology will reveal understanding itself as a basic existential state of human beings—precisely those who find themselves initially and always in a social and historical context, where scientific inquiry is only one mode of comportment toward their worlds. As such, understanding is a mode of our being human. A further mode of comportment to be disclosed, and indeed one implicit in the expression of scientific understanding, is the development of one's ontological understanding—an understanding not merely of entities in the world, but of the "worldhood" of the world, and indeed of one's own being there in the world as well. The essential possibility of working out this understanding will be characterized as "interpretation." And the concrete expression of such interpretation will be shown to be what I have called here "creative expression," the originary establishment of contexts of significance.

If Husserl's phenomenology was both descriptive in practice and creative as a method, that method needed further elucidation in a hermeneutical turn, taken by Heidegger, that must now become the object of my own hermeneutical analysis. For an account of an ontologically grounded primordial understanding, our attention must be turned to the *Daseinsanalytik* of Heidegger's *Sein und Zeit*. What comes to explicit expression through an act of discursive interpretation is there both the object of analysis and the phenomenon exhibited in the newly conceived phenomenological method. My own essay has since the beginning had that same dual purpose—to analyze and to exhibit the phenomenon of creative disclosure.

CHAPTER 4

Heidegger on Significance and Worldhood

In order for the "life-world," or some similar concept, to indicate the horizon for all meanings, indeed the universal context of significance, what is indicated thereby must accompany the first appearance of any particular signification as at once and unitarily already understood, even if only implicitly. As a primal meaning horizon, its origin cannot be accounted for by any process of synthesis or summation that commences with particular meaning intentions, such as for example Husserl's "elementary intentionalities." What can be reached through such procedures will always arrive too late to have been the horizon wherein the individual "elements" could have had their initial meanings in the first instance. Moreover, the proper execution of synthesis or summation will require a "blueprint" as its guide, and this would be an anticipatory conception of how all the "parts" fit together. That is to say, the elements will derive their meaning as parts of the whole from the original, and necessarily originary, conception that must in some way be understood in advance of adding them up. Even if this anticipatory conception is brought to explicit cognition only later, or indeed if it never reaches thematic clarity, still it is implicit from the first, seeing that some horizon of significance must be operative in order for any elementary intention to have a sense, and in order that such intentions may be synthesized into more complex meaning structures.

These considerations, which themselves anticipate the exposition to follow of Heidegger's teachings concerning significance and worldhood, where they are given ontological import, bring me back to my leading question: How in the first place does the shared understanding of the world arise? What is the origin of that communal understanding that is necessarily presupposed by any expression that communicates? Or, as it may now be put: How do we come to have that primal meaning horizon, called the "life-world" by Husserl, that stands under any particular act of communication and in its intersubjective character subtends any given language community?

The preceding inquiry into this issue was guided by the question, How is that understanding articulated? Directed to an exemplary phenomenon by this question, the investigation focused on the origin of the natural-scientific concept of the world, that is, "Nature," represented in the tradition by Galileo's texts, which were seen to illustrate the inventive establishment of a meaning horizon within which a shared understanding of physical nature has come to be systematically developed. The result was to see that creative expression, specifically a metaphor, lies at the origin of modern classical physics in which scientists merely attempted to read "the book of Nature." But this metaphor, as well as the intelligibility of the theoretical constructs subsequently developed by the institution committed to the methods and norms derived from it—namely natural science—implied the presupposition of a prior and more comprehensive shared understanding: one concerned with what Husserl termed the "life-world," which was grounded in the phenomenologist's attempt to read the essences of phenomena.

Even though this horizon functioned in Husserl's program at the last as the ultimate context of significance and allowed him to elucidate the basic concepts presupposed in Galilean science, his account of a synthetic constitution of the life-world was found incapable of finally grounding his own successful accomplishment, precisely because that synthesis, even as "passive," would require as its guide some preliminary conception of the whole. This inadequacy has in its turn been read as motivating a hermeneutical turn, by which phenomenology is carried beyond pure description of essences as well as beyond the uncovering of a merely ontic world, that is, a summation of entities.

The interpretive methods developed by Heidegger open the way for a phenomenological ontology that brings attention to bear on the *being* of entities in their significance, and in particular on the world as a relational totality, that is, in its capacity as a horizon of significance. In this newer program, inquiry begins with human existence revealed to itself in a context of significance—a context determined by this same disclosure and characterized ontologically as "the worldhood of the world."[1] Heidegger's existential analytic reveals this structure to be one of the items constitutive of being human. As a relational totality of involvements with which human beings are always already familiar, its origin is coterminous with the self-disclosing of human existence. In other words, the first, or indeed any, awareness of oneself is accompanied by an awareness of the world as the significant horizon in which one finds oneself.

To follow Heidegger's lead we must carry the preceding inquiry one step further. This step is initiated when we interpret the cardinal question, concerning the original emergence of an understanding of the world, as asking, Who discloses the world, so that it may be understood? Asked in this way, the answer is obvious: we who ask; we for whom an understanding of the world is both a possibility and an issue; but also, as will be illustrated in a subsequent chapter (Chap. 5), we who participate in originary acts of communication, for example, through producing or responding to the aesthetic expressions experienced in those works of art that most obviously set up "a world" of human significance.

When the question is approached this way, it becomes clear that the world asked about—indeed any world that can be asked about with the expectation of finding evidence for grounding our responses—is precisely correlative to our own possibilities for disclosing any region at all. In this sense the world *is* the region of human possibilities: it is uncovered as existing by our capacity to be affected by it and structured according to our capacity to understand whatever may affect us, while our comportment within it expresses the implicit understanding we always have of its worldhood.

Clearly, one of the possibilities within this region is to articulate systematically the understanding we have in regard to various ontic domains, as illustrated by the natural scientific tradition. Heidegger's contribution, relevant to the foundations of this practice, was to demonstrate the further possibility of systematically articulating our understanding of the ontological domain and to show how the latter possibility stands under the former. In either case, working out the possibilities of our understanding is what Heidegger called "interpretation," whatever mode of behavior might exhibit it, and when concretely realized in a discursive mode, it issues forth in explicit speech.

The task of clarifying and grounding these obvious answers to our cardinal question, however, requires that we escape the blindness to "meaning activity" that, as Husserl notes, is characteristic of objective-scientific thinking. It also requires that we go beyond Husserl's purely descriptive enumeration of entities, or "elementary intentionalities," whose ideal summation or synthesis is said to result in the concept of our world. In either case, the procedure is restricted to ontic inquiry; that is, priority is given to "elements" that are added together to produce meaning structures. Above all, the "who" of understanding must not be made inaccessible to investigation at the start by an inappropriate preconception of it, à la Husserl, as a transcendental ego, self-enclosed in a realm of pure subjectivity. Neither can we allow an initial separation between this "who" and the world understood, as is inherent to the Cartesian conception of an *ego cogito,* that is, a *subjectum* determined entirely by its *cogitationes.*

Rather, we must retain the unity of the phenomenon indicated by the new formulation of our leading question: we who disclose the world as the region of our possibilities, and the world that is the object of our understanding, are ineluctably bound together. The elucidation of either implicates that of the other. Heidegger indicates the structural unity of this phenomenon by hyphenating the name he gives to the basic condition of human existence: Being-in-the-world (*In-der-Welt-Sein*).[2]

I shall take Heidegger's existential analysis of human "disclosedness" as a map to guide the way around this hermeneutical circle, in an effort to make clear how the phenomenon called "worldhood" stands under the basic conceptions through which a scientific world, or indeed any other, is understood.

When we speak of the unitary phenomenon that has "human being" and "worldhood" for two of its structural items, and when a world is characterized as precisely correlative to the possibilities of human disclosiveness and thus already understood as the region of our possibilities, then it is evident we are not using the word *world* in the sense familiar to scientific discourse, nor indeed to objective thinking in general. As the reading of Galileo made clear, the objective-scientific "world"—more properly called "Nature"—is conceived as isolated from specifically human concerns; it is independent of human will, preestablished, and inexorable. Moreover, taken as the totality of all actual objects, or as in

Wittgenstein's definition, "all that is the case," the world cannot be brought to exhibit itself as a phenomenon. On this perspective only entities within the world, or strictly finite complexes of them, show themselves phenomenally, and their totality will be reached through an idealizing, projective synthesis. But we have used "world" to indicate the horizon of all meanings, the universal context of significance, and as such it must be capable, somehow, of showing itself as a unitary phenomenon, so that it will be understood prior to any synthesis. If utter confusion is to be avoided, the different sense of this term and their interconnections must be clarified, and the proper mode of access to what each indicates must be brought to light.

Heidegger distinguished four senses, two ontical and two ontological, that the word *world* may be used to express.[3] Two of these, one ontic and one ontological, are familiar to scientific discourse. In its first ontical sense *world* signifies just that totality of entities intended by objective thought, that is, the totality of those entities that can be individually inspected with regard to their own independent, objective properties. These properties will be discovered when the entities are made present in "just the way they look," that is, when they are inspected in the attitude proper to a spectator, as expressed by the root sense of *theoria.* In this attitude the observer will refrain from intervening in what is observed and will view the spectacle in isolation from any involvement with his own personal concerns that would give it a different character from what it is conceived to have objectively and in-itself. Galileo's experimental methods clearly were designed to uncover the "world of Nature" taken in this ontic sense, and the standard of objective, theoretical understanding upheld by the sciences ever since expresses the principle that the world so understood is one in which ideally the observer does not participate.

Although scientists do intervene, to the extent that they

alter the "natural state" of an entity during the course of experimenting with it, they do so methodically and for the purpose of discovering the characteristics of its unaltered state. This "objective" state will then be defined in terms of the standard conditions under which various alterations occur. Indeed, it was the recognition that the ideal of unobtrusive observation is on principle impossible to achieve, with respect to subatomic particles, that brought modern physics to its own internal crisis and established the principle of "uncertainty relations"[4] as one of the features distinctive of quantum mechanics as opposed to its predecessor. But this newer perspective, despite its revolutionary character, still retains as an ideal the unaltered state of a particle, even if its properties may be determined only probabilistically, and on the basis of the alterations brought about by the collisions inherent to observation of microparticles.[5] In either case, that is, in classical or quantum physics, as well as in physicalistic objectivism in general, the attitude of attending to the "world" taken in this first ontical sense is illustrated. Its entities are discovered by inspection, and their ideal totality is conceived through a projective synthesis.

Yet this ontic totality has its ontological counterpart, and correspondingly *world* is used in a second way, also familiar to objective thinking, in which the term refers to a relational totality. In this sense, the word signifies the structured realm in which the entities making up the ontic totality have their typical significance, for example, as being physical entities with determinable physical properties. But because *world* in this latter sense designates a relational rather than a mathematical totality, what it names will be understood in terms of its structuring principles; it will be interpreted in the explicit statement of these principles, and they cannot be reduced to mathematical functions. The entities belonging to this realm will indeed have a priori characteristics, or "essences": an entity lacking the proper essences simply will not belong to the designated "world."

For example, it is clear that the word may be used in this sense to speak either of the realm of all entities whatsoever, or analogously of any specific multitude, as in the phrase "the 'world' of a mathematician," where the realm of all possible mathematical entities is signified. This latter case illustrates the familiar use in which *world* indicates the context, or relational totality, whose concept must already be grasped prior to inspecting any entity within it for its own specific properties, precisely because the range of possible properties will be determined by the "world conception," and this will also determine the specific mode of inspection required for their discovery. Mathematical entities, for example, will be discovered by inspecting symbol arrays in which the sense of the individual symbols, as indeed the being of the entities they signify, will be determined by the structuring principles governing some particular system of functional correspondences, legitimating certain transformations while prohibiting others. That is, mathematical entities are determined by their functional properties within a given system. These entities will have their own proper being within the "world" that is comprehended by the principles determinative of its significance. Because *world* in this sense pertains to the being of entities, it is an ontological term; it gives us to understand just their "being present to inspection" in whatever specific mode is required, and their "being related" in accordance with the norms of the pertinent meaning horizon.

This distinction between the first ontic sense and the first ontological sense of *world* was anticipated in my earlier interpretation of Galileo's achievement as representing the codification of the a priori principles determinative of natural science's *investigandum.* His creative expression delineated the general structure of physical nature as a "world" in this ontological sense. It is now clear why that achievement had to be both creative and prescientific: inspection via experiment and observation uncovers only a finite series of entities; thus their totality—*world* in the ontical sense—lends itself only to *doxa*. But on the basis of his understanding that "the book of Nature" is universally ordered—the ontological sense—he could maintain that close observation, though finite, when conjoined with necessary, that is, mathematical, demonstration would reveal the quantitatively determinate structuring principles, or "laws of nature," in their necessary universality. Thus nature is made to yield itself to *epistémé* on the basis on an originary expression of the ontological conception.

Galileo's "assumptions," such as the preestablished order of nature and the universality of natural laws, thus are seen to be an expression, indeed an interpretation, of his prescientific understanding that physical nature is a "world," in this ontological sense. Once the conception of this universally structured realm was established among a community of investigators, but not until then, the way was opened for the institution of systematic inquiry, in accord with a priori methods, into an infinity of entities ordered by a priori categories. A member of any such category, taken merely as such, could be inspected with confidence that the results would be valid for all members of that category as such.

Not only are these two senses of *world* familiar to objective thinking, but this mode of thought also has its interpretation of their interconnection. From this perspective the structured realm must be grasped through constructive methods based ultimately on the results of inspecting particular entities for their objective properties; these properties will govern the manner in which objects may join together with others to form greater complexes or events, eventually and ideally to form the world. Because it is presupposed that entities in-themselves are what fundamentally exist, that the *atom* in the root Greek sense of the "indivisible" is what is ultimately real, and indeed that at bottom objective experience is based on particular physical objects, it follows that universal principles may be discovered only through induction; or, as viewed in the great experiment of logical empiricism, they will be "logically constructed."[6] Hence the world as a structured totality will come to be known only on the basis of a synthesis of elementary, or indeed "atomic," inspections.

On this view the procedure of scientific inquiry may properly be described as a "hypotheticodeductive method": any general principle is put forward as an hypothesis and its validity held in suspense until such time as its deductive consequences have been suitably observed. Whether verification or falsification is taken as the logically proper test, an understanding of the "world" in the ontological sense is held to be ultimately dependent upon an inspection of the "world" in the ontic sense. Because the objective-scientific view gives priority, in terms of both "knowing" and "being," to entities, it is characterized as ontical.

Yet despite the presupposition that inspection of present entities is the only reliable access to the "world of nature" or to any other actual world, Heidegger's distinction makes it clear that the ontological concept will have been operative from the beginning of any empirical investigation. Some guiding sense of the universal structuring principles, even if only in the mode of an "anticipatory conception," is required in order to know how to investigate what may be made present for inspection, and in order to make inductions or indeed to "logically construct the world." Within objective thought the priority given to entities, and hence to *inspection,* raises insurmountable difficulties for its own interpretation of the manner in which the conception of a universally structured realm is reached and "justified."

The epistemological crisis exhibited here is illustrated by a paradox evident within the prevailing "apprenticeship method" for training scientists. While this method brings trainees to an implicit grasp of their vocational world and inculcates within them the "scientific viewpoint," it contributes to the interpretation wherein the ontological sense of *world* is held to be necessarily posterior to the ontical sense.

A command of the former will appear to be attained only upon gaining mastery of the basic facts already established and the techniques practiced within the ongoing tradition. Yet these facts and techniques can have their proper sense only from the perspective of the "scientific viewpoint." Gaining this attitude indicates precisely a grasping of the ontological concept of science's "world." But because this concept is never brought to thematic clarity in scientific manuals, nor can the manner of originally obtaining it be elucidated by debates among those philosophers of science who adopt the standpoint of "naturalism," the successful apprentice is left to find that eventually he has somehow been indoctrinated with the proper viewpoint. Yet reflection will show that he was initiated into this understanding only through a process of training under mentors who in turn came by their own understanding in a similarly implicit manner. The regress evident here is not so much an indictment of this method of training in its practical pedagogical features as it is an indication that the principles of scientific thinking are themselves inadequate for interpreting the ontological foundations of the successful achievements—the recording of facts as well as the development of techniques—that are passed along within the tradition of science.

Once again Galileo's case is exemplary: his own commitment to experimental methods, and thus to inspection, prevented him from adequately interpreting the ground of his achievements. Because the structuring principles of physical nature could not themselves be first discovered by experimental means, but rather were required from the start in order for those methods to work, he quite honestly posited them as assumptions and deferred dealing with the impossibility of attaining their own verification a posteriori, that is, experimentally. But we can now see that these "assumptions" expressed his prescientific understanding of nature as a "world" in the ontological sense. This understanding reveals that some mode of access other than inspection was operative in the very birth of natural science, even though it could not be brought to light by Galileo's methods, and it continues to be operative for anyone who has attained the "scientific viewpoint," even while it is misinterpreted.

Heidegger called this overlooked mode of access "circumspection" (*Umsicht*[7]), because it is a mode of "sight" by which we look around and take in a structured whole. In it entities are uncovered not just in the way they look in-themselves, but rather in their significance, that is, as related to other items in the complex and to the complex as a whole. Indeed this being related in accord with the laws of nature "is" the *being* of entities insofar as they belong to the natural world. Manifestly an understanding of such being is implicit in Galileo's presentation of experimental methods, as well as in later expressions of the "scientific viewpoint." With the thematic exposition of this "sight" as belonging to the fundamental structure of human existence, Heidegger exposed our mode of access to the character of the natural world whereby it is understood as a relational totality—the character expressed metaphorically in Galileo's image of "the book of Nature."

By giving us to understand just such a relational totality, circumspection is the access that grounds in experience the principle of universal structure that Galileo, always the good scientist, was compelled to label an assumption and that he expressed by necessity in a "prescientific" mode of language. Husserl, for his part, also seeing that this experience does not satisfy scientific criteria, ascribed it to the prescientific natural attitude in which its results are characterized as doxic certainty of the typical style of the natural world as it emerges within the life-world horizon. But Heidegger recognized that the experiential access we have through circumspection is a genuine and original openness to a relational totality in its ontological character that he called "significance."[8] This ontological structure reached in circumspection is not, then, held as mere belief regarding the "style" of a synthetically constituted, that is, ontical, world as in Husserl's account. Nor is it posited as an assumption, required by experimental methods and apparently justified by their practical successes. On the contrary, *significance* is the general meaning horizon, which nevertheless is experienced personally in circumspection, that enables any belief or assumption to be posited significantly. On Heidegger's analysis, "significance," in its ontological import, names the ultimate ground for all significations, including basic scientific (ontic) concepts.

Through circumspection we are given to understand precisely this horizon that shows itself as the worldhood of the life-world, or indeed of any other—and this means the very characteristic of being structured into a world, which Heidegger later referred to in its active mood as "the worlding of the world."[9] As such, circumspection is our access to the ontological ground not only for scientific understanding but for life-world understanding as well.

By making thematic the notion of this access to worldhood, Heidegger was able to distinguish a second pair of senses *world* may be used to express—senses that Husserl tended to conflate in his use of the term "life-world." Although this concept functioned for Husserl as the ultimate meaning horizon, and as such prior understanding of it was implied by the occurrence of any elementary intentionality, his account of the life-world's constitution through projective synthesis resulted in a merely ontic totality that could only emerge "after" the original bestowal of meaning onto particular entities. Thus he was confronted with the same problem detected in Galilean science: where Galileo "made assumptions" with regard to the universal order and the uniformity of nature, Husserl invoked the notion of "doxic certainty" to characterize the prescientific thetic grasp of universal structuring principles, which then were to be "confirmed" (read "grounded") through phenomenological constitution. Circumspection, however, gives access to our worlds in their structured wholeness; ontologically it takes priority over inspection. And its acknowledgment allows Heidegger to overturn the inverted worlds posited by any merely ontic inquiry.

When Heidegger's ontic-ontological distinction—between entities and the being of entities—is brought to bear on the world as prescientifically understood, that is, on the life-world, it becomes clear that in its ontical sense the term *world* does not refer to entities made present to inspection, nor even to their synthetic totality. Rather in this sense it indicates the significant environment wherein an actual human being may be said to live, that is, the surrounding world in its capacity as a structure of meaning relations, whether this be the environment of his public life or that of his most personal existence.[10] As encountered in this "meaning environment" entities are initially familiar in their meanings, as these are determined by the functionality entities exhibit with respect to a person's concerns and aims for himself as well as those shared with his fellow men. Heidegger stresses the essential "meaningfulness" of such entities by giving them the collective designation "equipment" (*das Zeug*[11]), to be taken in the broad sense of whatever a person deals with while carrying out any endeavor. Whether the particular items function for him positively as "tools" or resist his efforts and emerge as obstacles to be surmounted, they are dealt with in terms of their sense (*Sinn*) within his own understanding of the significant situation.

Indeed, every "thing" is initially encountered in its significance within the overall meaning horizon, or world. Moreover, as bound up in a particular ordered totality, for example, "the workplace," individual entities remain inconspicuous so long as they serve their function; attention is directed through them to the aim of the project in which they are involved. Thus, knowledge of entities taken in this regard is properly and fundamentally expressed by "putting them to use," or, if need be, by replacing or repairing them, all with respect to their sense for the current project. Only in a derivative moment are they linguistically designated and made the bare objects of objective-scientific inspection.

As the region wherein human life takes place, the world is a "meaning environment"; it is a situation pregnant with sense. Within it things that matter to a person show themselves to be in the range of possible manipulation, to be used or to be avoided, in general to be dealt with. Because physical nature is literally the "ground" of our biological existence, it emerges within the world as a complex of entities that is particularly important, although not exclusively so. As necessary to survival, but not sufficient for human life, the natural world must be dealt with; this can be accomplished either "instinctively"—as our ancient forebears proved—or on the basis of knowledge gained systematically, for instance, through scientific inquiry, although in neither case is success guaranteed.

Likewise, languages in their inherited, historically established character emerge as communicative conventions that are to be dealt with, and these too may be manipulated on the basis of either implicit or explicit understanding. Yet even thematic investigation of languages may remain purely ontical, as all purely natural sciences do; it will remain so for as long as language is taken to be an entity merely encountered in the life-world and inspected as such, as long indeed as linguistic scientists fail to see that the conventions of discourse for expressing inherited thoughts—*Gerede*—derive originally from living, creative speech—*Rede*—which has its origins in the ontological structures of human existence. Indeed, all such ontical inquiries illustrate a mode of dealing with entities encountered in the world: the mode the Greeks called *theoria.* But in actual life men use languages as tools before inspecting them as objects in a cultural world, even as they derive sustenance from the natural environment before establishing "physical nature" as an object to be inspected by experimental methods.

Indeed, using language to communicate with others illustrates what it means to be involved in a world; it manifests a familiarity with the regional totality of the environment in its structured meaning character, as held in a shared understanding by all who are open to the communication. This character is expressed literally by the term "worldliness," that is, its being a world in the first place. Thus *world* in its second ontological sense signifies the worldhood of the surrounding life-world.[12] In this sense the term designates that relational totality of involvements with which any human existent is always familiar, toward which it comports itself, and out of which entities are encountered in their significance. Although ontically the "furthest" from us, ontologically worldhood is the "closest" to us because it is a structure of our own existence. For this reason it is overlooked as the ground of all our possibilities by any inquiry that commences with the adoption of physicalistic objectivism as its foundation.

As such, "worldhood" embraces in itself the characteristic both of a unitary phenomenon and of the universal context of significance within which entities may be significant. It is, then, the structured realm presupposed as meaning horizon in any particular signification, whether this occurs in relation to some special world, such as physical nature, or indeed to the life-world itself as the primordial meaning horizon.

Hence in this fourth sense of *world* distinguished by Heidegger, it names the ontological ground, originally given to understanding as a phenomenon through circumspection, on which the life-world in its ontical sense is understood. And within the horizon of this ontological understanding, entities that matter to human experience, whether in the mode of everyday practical concerns or in the systematic search for *theoria,* may be brought forth as entities "having" significance by assertions that point them out and characterize them. On this ground physical nature, for example, may be conceived as a preestablished, universally ordered material manifold that is amenable to mathematical formulation. Thus "nature" may be set before a community of inquirers in such a way that systematic methods for inspecting, and conventions for formally expressing, its structuring principles can be established and refined, even as Galileo's accomplishment and the tradition based upon it have demonstrated.

Yet as grounded in this universal context of significance, the ontical inquiry into physical nature must take its place alongside other possibilities for human comportment. However much natural science may stand out among these other human endeavors on ontical criteria, it derives its ultimate norms, as well as its very origin, from the same creative source: human being, which by disclosing the worldhood of the world establishes the horizon of possibility for all human actions and for all understanding.

By including circumspection in his interpretation, and making thematic the worldhood it gives access to, Heidegger inverted the priority relation assumed to hold between entities and world (that is, worldhood) by objective thinking. At the same time he reversed the priority given to elementary intentionalities in Husserl's account of the constitution of the life-world. Thus did he account for the function as original meaning horizon allotted to the life-world by Husserl, while elucidating the manner in which ontic inquiry first gains the implicit understanding of its *investigandum* as a structured whole, even though ontic concerns immediately cover over this wholeness. Because in circumspection we "look around" and "see" the orderedness of our environment, and the usefulness of entities within it, this "sight" gives original access to the world in its being a structured region, that is, in its worldhood. On this experiential basis we have the ontological understanding always presupposed by any inquiry that first posits an actual, structured manifold of entities.

With this interpretation of the interconnection between these various senses of *world,* Heidegger clarified Husserl's insight, namely that the basic concepts by which nature is scientifically understood are grounded in the life-world. And he did so precisely by bringing to light the manner in which the worldhood of the life-world is, in a single stroke, both phenomenally disclosed and primordially understood as the region wherein a human being dwells. This ontological understanding itself turns out to be a structural item essentially characterizing human existence; specifically, it is a constituent of human disclosedness, where together with the equally original "affectivity" and "discourse" it constitutes a human being's openness to the world—in any of the four senses.[13] On the basis of this openness to the worlds by which we are affected, we who understand them as such have the possibility of developing that understanding into an explicit expression via what Heidegger called "interpretation."

Because circumspection, in Heidegger's analysis, was disclosed as an original access to structured realms that reveals them in their worldhood, it is the pivot on which phenomenology itself turns from a description of essences to an interpretation of being—both that of worlds and that of entities within them. Husserl, however, was unwilling to follow his premier pupil in this turn, and the *Crisis,* which I have taken here as the best expression of Husserlian phenomenology, reveals that his conception of this method remains at the last essentially unmoved by the development it had been given in Heidegger's seminal work, *Being and Time,* even though the latter was published in Husserl's own *Jahrbuch* almost a decade before the composition of the *Crisis*.[14]

Significantly this last work from Husserl's pen did express a newly emphasized interest in the historical and intersubjective character of life-world understanding. But, in contrast to Heidegger's grounding of such understanding in the existential structures of human being, itself interpreted as essentially historical and social, Husserl retained the notion of a "transcendental constitution" as the "original formation of meaning."[15] His continued commitment to the methodological technique of transcendental reduction with its suspension of the issue of existence, and ergo to a transcendental ego "attached" to its intentional objects by the "universal a priori of correlation,"[16] compelled him to reject the ontological understanding that, on Heidegger's view, phenomenology not only can exhibit but, if it is to fulfill its own essential possibilities, must exhibit.

On Heidegger's newer conception of phenomenology, the failure to exhibit concretely this ontological understanding represents nothing less than the failure of phenomenology to understand itself. Ontological understanding, however, is possible only for those entities who are open to the world as an essential characteristic of their own existence, for example, human beings,[17] analyzed by Heidegger as those entities who find themselves in the world, with an understanding of it, already alongside the objects of their concern, and who are affected in their own being by that of their worlds. A transcendental ego, on the other hand, by virtue of its very conception, is from the start, and forever must remain, beyond such existential involvement in any world it might constitute. By thus reinterpreting its own "point of departure," while retaining the characteristic concern for "access," Heidegger's hermeneutical phenomenology represents a development, indeed a creative advance, over Husserlian descriptive phenomenology—insofar as the new interpretation can account for an "ontological understanding" grounded in the basic condition of human existence, but denied to a transcendental ego.

The full demonstration of Heidegger's newer conception of phenomenology clearly is the whole of *Being and Time* itself, where the way is prepared for "the question of Being" through a delineation and analysis of human existence as "a field where we can come to terms with [this question] in a way that can be controlled."[18] Even so, a useful summary of his principal innovations is evident in the preliminary characterization of what he understood by the term "phenomenology" found in the introduction to that work.[19] He makes explicit there his difference with Husserl by presenting phenomenology as precisely a *fundamental ontology*, even while he acknowledges the indebtedness to his mentor by stressing that the term "signifies primarily a *methodological conception*" that may be expressed by the Husserlian maxim "To the things themselves!"[20]

In this primary signification, that is, in its formal meaning, "phenomenology" does not designate the object of inquiry, and it does not characterize its subject matter; rather it indicates the manner of such research, while leaving indefinite which entities are to be taken as phenomena. In a turn of phrase reminiscent of Husserl, Heidegger says that the term informs us of the "how" with which this science treats whatever its theme may be. It expresses the norm according to which discussion will be restricted to what can be directly exhibited and demonstrated: as a methodological conception, phenomenology proscribes any sort of metaphysical speculation or idealizing substruction, such as Husserl detected in Galileo's "mathematization of nature." The Husserlian phrase "descriptive phenomenology," then, is pleonastic; yet as such it emphasizes the prohibition against characterizing anything without an appropriate demonstration. Although the standard of genuine access in any specific case will be determined by what the phenomenon is taken to be, in general the initial and ultimate appeal to evidence for the phenomenologist lies in *eliciting the phenomenon.*

But Heidegger goes beyond this negative definition of method, with its merely formal characterization of evidence, and interprets the two components of the term—*phenomenon* and *logos*—to show their inner relationship in a way that distinguishes this term from others formed out of the Greek in a like manner, such as *theology, biology, sociology.* Although "phenomenology" is superficially similar to these and on their model would be translated as "the science of phenomena," Heidegger's rendering of its components exhibits an essential interconnection that prevents a facile bifurcation into "science" and the name of a subject matter.

Although "phenomenon" may ordinarily be understood in a number of ways, all related to "appearance" or "mere appearance," from Heidegger's perspective its positive phenomenological sense signifies "*that which shows itself in itself,* the manifest."[21] Indeed any use of the term in the sense of "semblance," "disguise," or "illusion" will indicate a privative sense. Because of the reference relation inherent to this secondary sense, it will presuppose the fundamental signification that indicates what does the referring. Necessarily this must show itself in order for there to be any appearance that can be qualified by "mere," and indeed for any misapprehension to occur. But precisely because what is to become the phenomenon in the distinctive sense can remain hidden, and for the most part does so or is covered over by the assumption of inappropriate theory and by the inevitable addiction to "everyday" ontic concerns, there is the possibility for misapprehension. As a result phenomenology is needed as an explicit method for making manifest what can be made to show itself distinctively and fundamentally.

The *logos* in this term, then, is taken by Heidegger to signify precisely such "making manifest." It is interpreted as "discourse" (*Rede*), in the sense of expression that lets what the discourse is about be seen from itself.[22] As an ontological term "discourse" indicates the existential structural item belonging to human being that is the foundation of all expression. When realized in its fully concrete and specifically discursive mode, discourse is speech, and insofar as it is genuine, "*what* is said is drawn *from* what the talk is about."[23] In this mode "discourse" (*logos*) signifies verbal communication that brings to light in the discourse what has been hidden; it makes manifest to the listener what is "sighted" in the talk. Both parties to the communication are directed through the discourse to the phenomenon that is uncovered and characterized thereby. Thus the phenomenon as the manifest is always what *logos* as genuine discourse "lets be seen."

The formal meaning of "phenomenology," then, expressed in a typically Heideggerian phrase, is "to let that which shows itself be seen from itself in the very way in which it shows itself from itself."[24] Despite the striking repetitiveness in this expression, as Heidegger's etymological rendering through the Greek *apophainesthai ta phainomena* it describes with unerring precision what he conceived the task of phenomenology to be. By making explicit the interrelation between *phenomenon* and *logos,* as the names for "what is to be disclosed" and "the disclosing of that," this expression explicates the philologically proper translation, namely "science of phenomena," in such a way as to elucidate the inherent uniqueness of this science.

Moreover, its uniqueness is revealed even more clearly when the definition of "phenomenon" is deformalized by noting that in its distinctively phenomenological sense it indicates what "is *necessarily* the theme whenever we exhibit something *explicitly*": the *being* of entities.[25] And in Heidegger's view, this is "what phenomenology has taken into its grasp thematically as its object."[26] As such, with regard to its subject matter, this discipline may properly be called "the science of being": its name signifies our access to the theme of a genuinely grounded ontology, and it indicates the method for giving that theme demonstrative precision.

What is more, as fundamental ontology, this method of inquiry takes for its initial exemplary theme the entity that is ontologico-ontically distinctive, owing to its having "disclosedness" as a structural item essentially belonging to its manner of existence, namely human being. Because all inquiry is a mode of human comportment, the hermeneutical analysis of this entity is philosophically fundamental in that it lays out "the conditions on which the possibility of any ontological investigation depends."[27] And while establishing the foundations for ontological inquiry, this analysis becomes for the same reason also a hermeneutic of the foundations of the ontical sciences—those of "nature" as well as those of "spirit." In this way phenomenology is at the same time the "science" of the region that is ineluctably disclosed by any human comportment, that is, the world wherein human beings live, move, and have their being.

The interrelation of these two—*human being* and *world*—constitutes precisely that "field where we can come to terms with [the question of being] in a way that can be controlled."[28] It is the field wherein being is manifested and where it can be interpreted with demonstrative precision, which is to say, phenomenologically elucidated. Our own "being in the world" clears the openness wherein being gives itself to our understanding so that it may be interpreted in a manner significant to ourselves.

Even though Heidegger's phenomenological treatment in *Being and Time* restricts the interpretation of being to this field in which it is manifested to us and therefore treats being only insofar as it is "related" to human existence, nevertheless it elucidates the range of our possibilities as interpreters of being and indeed reveals our responsibility for keeping open this field wherein we are given to understand what it means for us and our worlds to be. For this reason, Heidegger was later to describe the fundamental task, and the ultimate destiny, of human being in his own metaphor as "the shepherding of being."[29] It is for our own sake, as well as for the sake of being, that we maintain our openness to the worldhood of the world, and that we work out our understanding of this region, which is at once the horizon of human significance and the ground for the possibilities of our ownmost human being.

If Heideggerian phenomenology fails to teach us "the meaning of Being in general"—and indeed by interpreting "interpretation" itself as a mode of human comportment that commences with what is already understood in the mode of an anticipatory conception with regard to whatever we have access to, Heidegger raises the doubt that the question of the meaning of "absolute" Being can even be posed meaningfully—nevertheless, the *Daseinsanalytik* teaches us our absolute relation to being, through which "there is" understanding, and on the basis of which our acts of *Dichtung* can bring it about that within a community of interpreters "there is" in fact ontological understanding.[30]

With its signification explicated in this manner, "phenomenology" can be seen to characterize philosophy's way of treating the object of ontology,[31] and because this object is necessarily presupposed by any inquiry that intends to exhibit its theme explicitly, it is the theme that is philosophically fundamental. For these reasons Heidegger says, "Philosophy is universal phenomenological ontology."[32] It takes its departure from the interpretation of human existence, and this makes "fast the guiding-line for all philosophical inquiry at the point where it *arises* and to which it *returns*."[33]

By describing as well as demonstrating the way this circle of interpretation may be traversed, Heidegger had already exhibited in *Being and Time* the way in which philosophy, as itself a mode of our being in the world, can heed the challenge Husserl was to issue some years later: to regain its original status as "universal science" and as genuine "first philosophy."[34] Both its point of departure and that for the sake of which philosophy is undertaken lie in human existence. We who have already uncovered the being of the world through our own *disclosedness* and who manifest our understanding of its worldhood by our concernful dealings in it have the possibility of making that understanding explicit, so that our own ontical existence may be shaped by our ontological understanding.

The universal task of phenomenology is to lay out this understanding with demonstrative precision, and through such interpretation to give thematic clarity to our basic familiarity with the being of ourselves, of our worlds, and of the entities encountered there. Conceived in this way phenomenology is tantamount to "first philosophy," although now secure in its method and in the access to its theme. As such it offers the possibility for performing the grounded interpretation of man and his world required by the Greek conception of mankind's freely shaping its existence through ideas of reason.

If the ontic-ontological distinction—between entities and their being, between "world" and "worldhood"—enabled Heidegger to exhibit the primordiality of ontological understanding, not only as a possibility for *theoria* but as an existential structural item constitutive of being human, then three dimensions of ontological problematics that must be kept distinct emerge: (i) the being of entities that are proximally encountered, in their usefulness or involvements, through circumspection—called *Zuhandenheit*; (ii) the being of entities that are made present to inspection by taking them out of the relational totality where entities are first encountered—called *Vorhandenheit*; and (iii) the being of that relational totality itself, which makes it possible for entities to be encountered at all—the "worldhood of the world."[35] The first two kinds of being pertain only to entities that do not have the uniquely human manner of existing; indeed these entities will manifest one or another kind of being appropriate to them according to the assignment given them by human concern within the relational totality of worldhood. Heidegger reserves the term "categories" for the universal concepts pertaining to these first two manners of being, and he introduces "*existentials*" (*Existenzialien*) for the analogous *explicata* appropriate to analyzing human existence structures.[36]

It is the third kind of being that is a constitutive item in human structures: "worldhood" is an existential. And because we are given to understand it in our operative understanding of ourselves as having possibilities within this existence horizon, we can understand entities that are categorially explicated either as functioning in relation to our *praxis* or as merely lying before our theoretical interests to be inspected as such. As the context of significance with which any actual human being is already familiar, worldhood provides the shared meaning horizon for all significations, and hence for all communication. Our primordial familiarity with this horizon is manifested by our concernful dealings within it. Even so, in one mode of such comportment, namely the manipulation of verbal conventions, and specifically in philosophical and scientific discourse directed to the end of thematic explication of how it is that we can communicate, this familiarity has repeatedly been hidden. And it has been obscured, or at best disparaged, in large part because categorial explication—ontic analysis—has been taken to be primary.

By means of this threefold distinction within the problematics of ontology, Heidegger brought to light the necessity for commencing that inquiry with what we are rather than with what we are not.[37] For it is only through an elucidation of human existence-structures that our genuine mode of access to entities in their being may be thematically secured and thus established as a methodological norm for any investigation of our worlds—including the investigations performed by the ontic sciences.

All merely natural sciences are purely ontic in conception and in execution; they inquire into what we are not. Even when the topic of "man" is finally admitted into their *investigandum,* for example, in the disciplines of physiology, anthropology, psychology, and sociology, this theme is preconceived on the category of "substance." The criteria of scientific objectivity, established in accord with the notion of substance, dictate that inspection will provide the fundamental evidence to support any given explanation. Thus these sciences can treat "human beings" only to the extent that we share a range of characteristics with entities lacking the distinctively human manner of existing, primarily those we possess by virtue of being physical organisms. The distinctive features of what we are must remain problematic, if they are seen at all, in any inquiry that takes the guiding conception of its theme from precisely that which we are not.

On the contrary, phenomenological ontology as conceived by Heidegger is grounded in human familiarity with a structure of its own being—worldhood—and this provides an existential way of determining the nature of human existence. By commencing with an inquiry into what we are, phenomenology turns aright the inverted world taken as philosophy's theme ever since Plato and Aristotle established "substantiality" as the exemplary mode of being and attempted to interpret everything, including human being, on its model. With "substance" posited as fundamental to *ta onta*, phenomenal examples could be randomly selected from "things," and for the most part these were chosen on the basis of simplicity, presence, and endurance. Accordingly human existence did not come to be investigated until after the conceptual patterns that set the norms for all interpretation were formulated. Hence, when human being was treated, predictably it raised notorious difficulties, and these have persisted ever since in the philosophical tradition, whence they have been passed along to the scientific tradition.

In turn, these difficulties have become embedded in our languages to such an extent that a philosopher working in the modern era who would overturn the traditional prejudice in favor of "substance" as the universal fundament must free his thought from the conceptions that are sedimented in our languages; thus, to the extent that he succeeds, his own expression must exhibit a creative use of language, at times literally wrenching it out of its customary paths, as Heidegger's own text amply illustrates.

As we have noted, Heidegger's analysis of what we humans are uncovers significance as the ontological ground for signification. But further, with particular relevance to what has become our continuing example, namely natural scientific inquiry, his analysis of worldhood exhibits those of its structures from which the essential conception of a scientific world are derived. It is for this reason that Heidegger's phenomenological, that is, ontological, grounding for the scientific concepts of space, time, and history is given in existential terms as human spatiality, temporality, and historicity, those ontological structures that remain furthest away in that they have been continually covered up by the scientific concern with space, time, and history.

If the structures of our distinctively human being may be hidden by centuries of misguided philosophical discourse, then our mode of philosophizing must undergo a radical change. I shall illustrate this change in mode by looking not at our scientists as paradigms of those who know, but at our artists, who may, perhaps, be seen to offer a better example yet of persons creating a unique significance via their concern for communicating something of how their worlds turn. For in the artist's quest we gain some sense of the commitment to the struggle with available materials to express the worlding of one's own world. In particular, when a painter such as Cézanne makes visible on his canvases the spatiality of his world, he brings to expression for all of us a personal experience of our shared meaning horizon and thus reveals the ontological basis for the ontic concept of a public space.

From Galileo and Husserl then, I shall move to Cézanne, and from Heidegger to Merleau-Ponty, who was as much perplexed by "Cézanne's doubt" concerning the validity of his perceptions as was Husserl by the crisis in the sciences that was generated by Galileo's criticism of the Peripatetics. I make this turn to investigate how the worldhood of his world governs what significance may be created even in the painter's world.

CHAPTER 5

The Book of Nature Read by Cézanne

According to the familiar Galilean dictum, the book of Nature is written in the language of mathematics. On the basis of this conception modern science is committed to reading nature in terms of formal quantitative functions. With the benefit of Husserl's analysis of Galileo's mathematization of nature, it is evident that the language of mathematics pertains to the perceptually experienced world only indirectly, and through the mediation of an ideally constructed conceptual model. In modern natural science, Husserl says, "we measure the life-world . . . for a well-fitting *garb of ideas* [*Ideenkleid*]."[1] Indeed, Galileo himself was aware of the need to abstract from the qualitative richness of the perceived world in order to interpret nature's structures in quantitative terms. Still he and his compatriots in classical science, as Merleau-Ponty has said, "clung to a feeling for the opaqueness of the world, and . . . expected through [science's] constructions to get back into the world."[2] From a perspective on this broader context defined by the aims of experimental inquiry, the commitment to the language of mathematics can be seen to have already set the task of returning to the life-world, if science were indeed to be an interpretation of man's own environment.

But when the principal language in which its interpretation is expressed inherently hides nature behind a veil of ideal constructions, the imposed task of subsequently unveiling what has thus become hidden requires an entirely different mode of expression—one that would permit a reading in the same terms as those in which nature is originally experienced. On the conception of the art of painting that emerges from the achievements of Paul Cézanne, as both artist and theorist of art, creative acts of painting supply us with examples of this sought-after mode of expression.

According to Cézanne, who has come to be recognized as the towering figure marking the beginning of the modern era in the tradition of his medium,[3] a painter is engaged, no less than a scientist, in the effort "to read [the book of] Nature." Yet rather than abstracting from its perceptual immediacy and interpreting nature through a conceptual language such as mathematics, or even through imagination, which he said replaced reality in the pictures by the old masters, Cézanne devoted his efforts to "realizing" his motifs in such a way that he could describe his act of painting as "attempting a piece of nature."[4] His understanding of the painter's medium not only compelled him to think precisely in terms of visual experience but allowed his interpretation to be expressed in the very same terms through which nature was revealed to him: what he called "sensations of color."

Whatever is deemed to be the proper language for describing the relations between such "sensations," Cézanne's commitment to a "primary language" that appeals to our perceptual sense enables his works to speak with the same degree of immediacy and directness as does nature in our primary experience of it. Thus he retains the possibility of presenting a piece of nature in an expression that is free of the detour through ideal conceptual models unavoidably introduced into a scientific interpretation by the language of mathematics. His interpretations of nature can produce that prior visual tension, systematically abandoned in Euclid's conceptual science and distrusted as subjective in mathematical physics, which remains in all actual perceptions as an "essential" stratum of the experience of seeing, however commingled it may be with verbal and conceptual strata. By working in a medium that appeals to this innocent stratum of experience, Cézanne also retains the possibility of recalling our attention to perceived nature as the initial environment of our lives; he may teach us, then, how to regain the direct contact with our natural world, in its native significance, that is lost or deferred when in scientific sophistication we take an ideal, mathematized "nature" to be the "real" world.

In the practice of his art, Cézanne was brought to confront nature in all its qualitative richness and opaqueness. He did so with a vision that was not blinded by the conceptual constructions that give geometric thought its ideal clarity; nor, indeed, was his vision distorted by the habits of "practical" thought in which familiar items are glanced at only in order to be identified and re-cognized, but are seldom truly seen. And in the almost desperate explanations of what he was attempting, voiced only late in his life when it became apparent that he would be unable to complete the difficult works needed to "prove the theories—which in themselves are always easy,"[5] he struggled to formulate the conception of painting that was to be so influential after his death. Despite the conflicts that may be found between his theory and his practice, and despite the departure from "reading nature" taken by following generations of painters,[6] Cézanne showed how the painter's art could present to perceptual experience the original emergence of nature into a significant order, and in doing this, he taught us how to recapture the primary world that Galilean science first presupposes and then conceals.

As a result of Cézanne's achievements, the definitive character of the painter's art may be seen to lie in its essential visual immediacy, and its guiding aim, to be the exercise of its inherent possibilities for disclosing a world purely through visual means. Despite his own agonizing self-doubts, partly motivated by the consistently negative responses from the official art establishment of his time, Cézanne's "studies" on canvas and his formulations of theory offer a genuine education in seeing the world as if for the very first time.

If Cézanne's lesson is ever to be learned, what he offered to sight through the practice of his métier must first be seen, and talked about, if at all, only afterward. For obviously, when dealing with painting, as with any visual medium, it is fatal to ignore the visibility of what is seen. Regard then his *Mont Sainte-Victoire Seen from Les Lauves*.[7] Surely this is one of the more fully "realized" studies among his many attempts featuring this now familiar massif, even though this study too remains "unfinished" by his own critical standards.

It takes little imagination to recognize the roofs of a farmstead rising out of the surrounding trees in the foreground, a straight road on the right passing behind the trees in the center, and a patchwork of fields interspersed with foliage receding toward the horizon where the distant mountain thrusts its flattened peak into the clouded sky. But to attend to these familiar objects, or even to the "aerial perspective" of their layout, is precisely to attend to what is general. It is to imagine, to re-cognize, that is, to divert attention from the visible to the conceptual, and to remain open to vision only long enough to categorize the objects and the experience under already available ideas. Categorial thought will pass over the perceptual experience offered here, and the origin of concepts in our openness to the actual world through perception will remain obscure.

The important question here is not what is represented, but how what we are given to see is presented on the surface of our visual field, whatever familiar concepts may be found useful in a subsequent description. In order to appreciate the innocent, nonsophisticated, noncritical sort of visual experience this painting offers, it is necessary to defer for a moment the tendency to name and conceptualize and thus to geometrize the objects of vision. It is necessary to place in abeyance our cultured habits of thought so as first to see and to think purely in visual terms. If, as Cézanne said, painters "must render the image of what we see, forgetting everything that existed before us,"[8] viewers of their works must also suspend what they "know" while vision performs its primary function, and that is to reveal our world at a distance.

In short, what is called for is a practice similar to the methodological procedure Husserl labeled *epoché*: the suspension of what is held to be true "objectively," of what is "known" conceptually, in order to focus attention on what is intended in a first-order act of awareness. Husserl, we recall, was concerned to refine this notion and to establish it as a first methodological principle of phenomenology, indeed as a general philosophical procedure. As fully developed into the method of his transcendental phenomenology, it led him to a transcendental ego in relationship to its intentional object, the ordinary life-world of the subject. But Cézanne, who had already learned to perform a sort of "bracketing" in the practice of his art, was interested only in reducing to the level of a strictly embodied act of awareness, that is, to pure perceptual experience, the first-order act befitting a painter. The procedure he was content to describe simply as "forgetting" is, then, more closely akin to Merleau-Ponty's adaptation of the Husserlian device; for in Merleau-Ponty's "philosophy of embodiment" the final attainable reduction leads to a conscious body engaged in animating its perceived world. Whatever differences eventually arise from the philosophers' development and application of this procedure, for the moment it is enough to see that the initial impulse is basically the same: the aim of suspending, or forgetting "everything that existed before us," is to obtain a current awareness

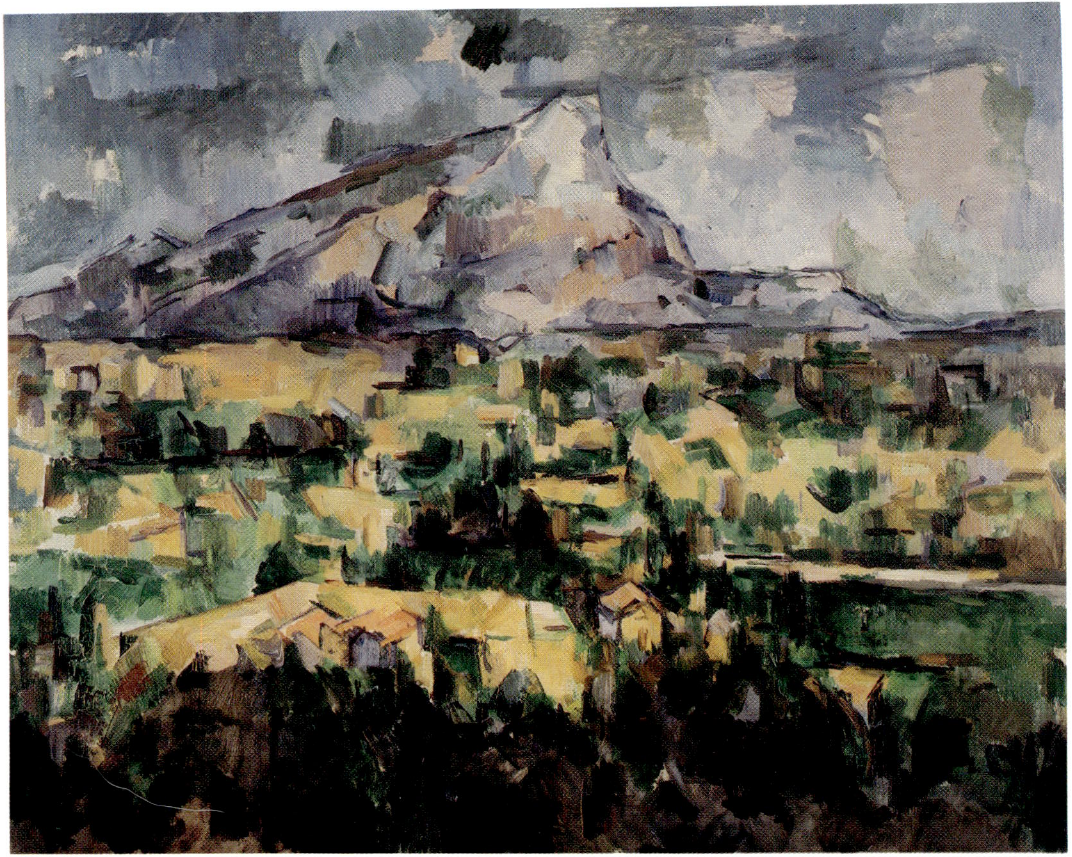

Paul Cézanne, *Mont Sainte-Victoire Seen from Les Lauves*, 1902–1904, oil on canvas, 27½ inches by 35¼ inches. The Philadelphia Museum of Art: George W. Elkins Collection. Reproduced by permission.

of what now "exists" before us, taken precisely in the way it shows itself.[9] For the painter, as well as for anyone who would experience his work, what must be made the object of present attention is the visible purely in its visibility. The painter's *epoché*, according to this interpretation, reduces the real objects of nature to their sheer visibility.

In the case of the *Mont Sainte-Victoire,* what is presented to sight is a composition executed in shades of violet, ocher, green, and blue. Strong contrasts of bright-obscure and warm-cool, and the dissonance of specific hues give the light an intense vibrancy. Shimmering in the streaks and patches that dominate the texture, this light suppresses any sharp delineation of detail and subverts the discovery of order by any but a "global" view that first takes in the structural whole. From such a perspective, a rhythm that controls the vigorous conflicts and orders the underlying chaos of sensations in an undeniably dynamic resolution may be noted. The clashing sensations coalesce before the eye, spontaneously and as if by magic, into a harmony that opens an ordered space in which vision is quite at home, even while it is never allowed to become stagnant.

The predominant tensions set up within this overall harmony may be indicated by considering the picture plane to fall into three horizontal sections. These, of course, are abstractions, as indeed "picture plane" is, and serve only to economize a description of the organization within which Cézanne's modulations of colors reveal the deep space in which objects appear precisely where and how they are seen: in the distance and yet near.

In the bottom section sharp contrasts dominate: light against dark, warm against cool, violet against a noncomplementary green. The chromatic progression of bright ocher radiates against the amorphous streaks of obscure violet. Balanced by the lighter green patches on each side, the violet and ocher mass presses toward the center and rises through a dark-light-dark rhythm into a verticality that is more clearly established in the finely articulated building near the top of a low hill.

In the uppermost section the contrasts are subdued, but here the progression within the blue tonality and the sweeping contour lines produce a dramatic verticality culminating in the highlighted, sheer face of the mountain's peak. Again the mass is concentrated in the center, but this time it is molded into a single, irregular pyramid that is brought forward by the negative spaces on either side. On the left, two converging diagonals delineate the positive space of the mountain's twin ridges and gently divide it from the rather flat sky above. But on the right, the more abrupt profile gains special fullness from its juxtaposition with the airy, almost infinitely distant sky framed by its contour.

The middle section is given over to a vibrant and indeterminate patchwork of colors that spreads horizontally into the periphery of vision and marks the transition between the seen and the unseen. Here texture, devoid of any definite structure, vibrates in muted colors showing quite accurately what appears beyond the focal areas of the visual field. Yet, in this case, the peripheral zone is made also to lie between two more definitely located structures, at once separating them, holding them together, and helping to place them. As the indefinite middle distance, it is the span across which the near and far verticals compete for dominance.

The predominant tension, then, into which these vigorous conflicts are resolved is a push/pull between the low hill in the foreground and the distant mountain. The hill and farmstead, seen from above, are brought near by strong contrasts and overlapping verticals, while the boldly structured mountain rises through eye level and is carried off into the distance by gentle shadings in the rich-blue to pale-violet range of coloration. Yet even at its distance, the solidity of the mountain is revealed by the progression of light on its near face, and by the greater distance of the sky, especially the portion receding behind its abrupt right profile. Bound together yet separated by the indeterminate flat plain, these two vertical structures compete for the center of focal attention.

Finally, the many complex modulations of color are organized for a global vision so as to open up a space into which that vision is stretched. The farmstead and the mountain are each revealed at a distance, yet they "flee toward a centre on our horizon" described by Cézanne as a "culminating point," the point of each object that is always "the closest to our eye."[10] Standing on the surface of our visual field, these objects exert a tension between the near focus and the distant focus, giving us to feel explicitly the stretch that vision itself is in our primary experience of seeing. The space of the "life-world" is made visible in this "piece of nature" by its organization of color so as to give us the sensation of distance that initially establishes our experience of space. If the objects retain a certain unfamiliarity, and if nature is not represented here as we "know" it to be, that is because Cézanne has presented space as something to be seen in an experience that underlies the conception of space, whatever geometric abstractions may subsequently prove useful for conceptualization and its purposes.

In this painting, then, Cézanne has revealed how it is that vision traverses an indefinite gap to hold objects at a distance, and by its stretch opens a space wherein things may emerge to stand over against us, distant and yet near. In the concentric waves of this visual space, objects are seen in their roundness as well as in their "aroundness." Cézanne's interpretation of nature, expressed here through an organization of the immediate sensations of colors, makes explicit our placement in space, and indeed our own "creative" involvement in its being thrown open around us.

The sector of the environing world, here exhibited in the process of its spontaneous formation into an ordered arrangement, will lend itself to intersubjective description and eventually to geometrical analysis. Yet in this stage of its revelation, the only standards for measuring it remain perceptual; they are the perceived distances lying between here and there, wherein the objects are only just coming into stable location. This is a land that can be metered only by sight. Indeed, if we look closely—across the visual indeterminateness of the "middle distance"—we can see how far beyond the farmstead lies the base of the mountain. In this way we first come to have a familiar reference for gauging what is meant by the surveyor's "eighteen kilometers." Indeed, the more significant units here would be "a stone's throw" or "a morning's walk."

Because of its sensuous immediacy and qualitative richness, this landscape arrests us at the level of visual experience; seeing it is somewhat unsettling to our accustomed manner of quickly conceptualizing what we see. A quantitative interpretation seems barren and strangely remote, even when we know of the practical and technological benefits of the precision and clarity belonging to mathematical language. By offering a view of nature in its originally perceived spatial expanse and by retaining it ambiguities, Cézanne has presented to vision the world that is veiled behind the conceptions required in a mathematical interpretation. His interpretation, on the contrary, speaks directly to perceptual consciousness. It teaches us to read the book of Nature in a language inherently understood by vision. Indeed, it gives us to understand nature as it is experienced in its prescientific, premathematical, and preconceptual yet nevertheless meaningful structures, that is, as originally seen.

Cézanne's refusal to abandon the sensuous surface of nature enabled him to present a world unfamiliar to thought grown comfortable with the ideal clarity of conceptual models. And yet, in his departure from the abstractions of categorial thought he did not abandon the volumetric relations so coldly schematized in geometric diagrams. Instead he built up those volumes by organizing "patches of color" so as to present for our visual experience the space of the life-world in all its sensory richness, in its presence and plenitude and imprecision—qualities that Merleau-Ponty will say give the perceived world its mark of actuality. Cézanne's commitment to the opaque world of primary experience and his appeal to "innocent" vision, however, do not reflect a "primitivism" in the usual art-historical sense. He has not abandoned the deep space, the volumetric sense of our surrounding world, that in geometry and linear perspective are represented by diagrams requiring conventions of interpretation. Nor has he ignored particular knowledge of his motif's "abstract structures," such as the underlying geological formation of the landscape. And clearly he has not disregarded what he learned during many hours spent studying the masters in the Louvre—in his phrase, "the book from which we learn to read."[11] But, by finding a way to present the deep spatial expanse that shows on the sensuous surface of our world, while avoiding the detour through a purely conceptual realm, Cézanne has confronted the sciences, as well as art history and art theory, with the visible nature that they refer to only mediately.

Mont Sainte-Victoire Seen from Les Lauves is only one of many now well-known paintings that demonstrate the confident mastery of his craft Cézanne attained in his maturity, despite the doubt displayed in his writings when he attempted to verbalize an intellectual understanding of what he had achieved. Surely this work confirms that a painting can satisfy his thesis that "art is a harmony which runs parallel with nature."[12] And if we are taught by it to see in an innocent but genuine manner that is discredited in our scientific sophistication, then it fulfills his desire "to produce pictures that will be an education."[13] And yet, as the letters from his final years clearly show, Cézanne remained dissatisfied with his progress, and he seriously doubted that he would ever prove the theories by which he attempted to explain his lifelong quest. The letters and reported conversations leave no question that a disparity existed between what he had achieved and what he aspired to—between his practice and his theory. Although he obviously longed for public and official recognition of his accomplishments, the higher and more troubling standards were those he projected for himself, and these applied only to his own perspective on his "studies."

This disparity may, perhaps, be clarified by considering it as resulting from the conflict between two media of expression: (i) linguistic expression, which is inherently replete with sedimented meanings and "metaphysical" conceptions, and (ii) an artistic medium such as painting, which in Cézanne's hands became a means for directly and creatively expressing the personal struggle to achieve a sense of order out of what was given to his own experience of our surrounding world. In this context, Cézanne's verbal expressions of theory exhibit an implicit adoption of the Galilean conception of "strict reality."

The two constant themes of his stated purpose were "to possess sensations" and "to read nature." The meaning of these for him and their role in his harsh self-judgment become comprehensible in the light of two aphoristic "opinions" on the painter's art, transcribed and published by Émile Bernard after conversations with the reclusive artist.

According to one of the "opinions":

> To read nature is to see it, as if through a veil, in terms of an interpretation in patches of color following one another according to a law of harmony. These major hues are thus analyzed through modulations. Painting is classifying one's sensations of color.[14]

This is precisely what we found in the *Mont Sainte-Victoire*—patches of color modulated according to a law of harmony so as to interpret nature as it reveals itself in the space opened up by vision. The landscape there is seen "as if through a veil," that is, through the shimmering light presented on the surface of our visual field by the colors, or in Merleau-Ponty's phrase, through "the vibration of appearances which is the cradle of things."[15] This notion of a veil is, perhaps, what was retained from his sojourn with the Impressionists, and especially with Pissarro. Yet this statement, as well as his canvases, exhibit Cézanne's insistence on recapturing the volumetric object in deep space that gives the "reality" to perceptual experience in its penetration of the atmosphere and light that so captivated the Impressionists. Unlike them he was not content to paint the veil; his sensations of color were classified so as to paint the solid nature made visible through its sensuous surface or, better, made visible by the tensions felt within the harmony of that sensuous surface.

In one of his last letters, written to his son, Cézanne gives a clue to why he found fault with his interpretations of nature: a disparity between the intensity of nature's own colors and those of his canvases remained. His predilection for comparing one with the other is made clear in the following:

> I must tell you that as a painter I am becoming more clear-sighted before nature, but that with me the realization of my sensations is always painful. I cannot attain the intensity that is unfolded before my senses. I have not the magnificent richness of colouring that animates nature.[16]

Whereas we see a vibrant radiance in the *Mont Sainte-Victoire,* achieved through the bold juxtaposition of dissonant colors and sharp contrasts, Cézanne saw an even greater brilliance when he turned from the canvas to look across the plain at the distant mountain. He aspired to create a harmony "parallel with nature" and in no way inferior to it; yet in comparison with the sensations felt before the motif, those produced by his paintings were lacking in vividness. His studies remained interpretations that were subordinate to what he would present, as indeed any interpretation, by virtue of its dependent character, will inevitably be.

Cézanne was caught in the contradictory stance of affirming the independent reality unfolded by his paintings and at the same time comparing them with the immediate sensations given by nature, taken as the visible world "outside" the paintings. Although his achievements laid the foundations for the later full recognition that a painting is a truly independent visual structure, in his word a genuine "piece" of the visible world, in that it opens its own space and possesses its own degree of internal intensity, the pioneer of this conception was not yet radical enough in his theory to dispense with comparisons, even though his own practice tended to subvert them.

In another of his aphoristic "opinions" he implied the endlessness of his project deriving from the developing interaction between sensation and thought that forms the basis for originary expression.

> There are two things in the painter, the eye and the mind; each of them should aid the other. It is necessary to work at their mutual development, in the eye by looking at nature, in the mind by the logic of organized sensations, which provides the means of expression.[17]

It is obvious that these two "faculties" were coupled when Cézanne took brush in hand and painted; yet they seemed unequally developed and divided against one another when he spoke of his work and attempted to explain in words what he was seeking.

Cézanne's dissatisfaction reveals his inability to conceptualize the unity of eye and mind, even while the results of his primary means of expression show vividly his command of their unity. Indeed, his paintings make abundantly clear the unity of eye and mind in his own openness to the visible world, a unity that finds expression through his hand. Eye, mind, and hand—abstracted designations for the interdependent functions of a single living body—were joined in the mastery of one means for interpreting his world, even if his lingual expression failed to reach the same level. Only on the basis of such unity could he have interpreted nature in a manner that presents so clearly and directly to our experience the spatiality by virtue of which we have a world surrounding us at a distance.

However it is conceived by geometers, we perceive the space created in *Mont Sainte-Victoire* as a series of modulated color tonalities. And if Cézanne's reading of the book of Nature is more accurate than Galileo's, the reason seems obvious: the painter displays the spatiality of his world on the surface of his expression and in so doing retains the sensuous immediacy of his lived world, whereas the scientist abstracts from the vibrancy and sensuous quality of the lived world and projects a theory that, in its idealization, gives us space as something to think.

According to Merleau-Ponty, who has criticized the dilemma of Cézanne's doubt, the creation and appreciation of paintings most clearly exemplify the relative roles played by "the eye" and "the mind"—by a radical empiricism on the one hand and a vigorous rationalism on the other—in our cognition of space.[18] In what follows, I shall be concerned with Merleau-Ponty's predilection for the primacy of perception in our reading of the book of Nature.

"Cézanne's difficulties are those of the first word," according to Merleau-Ponty's explanation of the troubled painter's predicament.[19]

> Because he returns to the source of silent and solitary experience on which culture and the exchange of ideas have been built in order to know it, the artist launches his work just as a man once launched the first word, not knowing whether it will be anything more than a shout.[20]

Having first suspended what he had learned from science and the museums and society, Cézanne then confronted the task of recapturing the structure of the perceived world and making it visible in its original emergence into a significant order. Because he sought to paint this "primordial world," what he expressed could not be "the translation of a clearly defined thought, since such clear thoughts are those which have already been uttered by ourselves or others."[21] The meaning he wanted to express was not available anywhere until his creative act brought it to view. Before he had made it visible, he could only question the inchoate significance emerging on his canvas.

In the realm of authentic expression, "conception" cannot precede "execution," Merleau-Ponty has written[22]—a reminder for us of Nietzsche's dictum that what is *gedacht* cannot precede what has been *gedichtet*.

The depth of Cézanne's uncertainty indicates to Merleau-Ponty the degree to which he bracketed the "already constituted reason in which 'cultured men' are content to shut themselves" and struggled to impose on his world an originary sense from the standpoint of "a reason which contains its own origins."[23] From this standpoint, freed from inherited habits of thought, he had no guarantee of success. Only his act of expression, by establishing its own context of significance and by eliciting an understanding response, either from himself in the future or from other perceivers, would prove that his initially vague intimation of a significance had indeed pointed to a realizable meaning.

Cézanne's doubt, Merleau-Ponty says, derived from the purpose of his work. In this he was not content to paint at second hand, "linking old ideas in a new way and . . . presenting forms that have been seen before."[24] He was intent on making paintings that would awaken the experiences in which ideas have their roots and would convey the "sensations" through which his world was displayed before his very eyes. Having returned to a most personal contact with his own world, he could do no other than launch his work from the base of his own freedom and then endure the accompanying uncertainty. For the act of expression finds its resolution only in the approval of other equally free individuals; if that act is genuinely originary, the response cannot be calculated in advance. Yet when it does "come to life for other people . . . the work of art will have united these separate lives."[25] The painter's world will then be shown to be our world also, and his brave act of expression will have established a basis on which the rest of us can communicate in our "cultured" secondhand expressions. The uncertainty Cézanne felt is endemic to creative expression, because its charge is to set forth, for the first time, the horizon whose shared understanding links inherently free lives.

In this way the case of the Provençal artist served as a clear example for Merleau-Ponty, who sought to reawaken an awareness of the nonreflected (*l'irréfléchi*) and to clarify its role as the grounding connection between reflection (read "philosophy") and the actual world. This is the task begun in his *Phenomenology of Perception*,[26] where he attempted, as he said later, "to define a method for getting closer to present and living reality."[27] Although this method was derived from Husserlian descriptive phenomenology, when Merleau-Ponty performed the series of *epochés* he arrived in the final attainable reduction, not at a "transcendental ego" and its intentional object, but at a correlation between a living conscious body and its perceived world. Thus the focus of his investigation was on "man's relation to perceptible reality and . . . man's relation to others on the level of perceptual experience."[28] It is in the context of these two relations that he found Cézanne's achievements in the act of painting, as well as the dilemma of his doubt, to be so illustrative.

Because Merleau-Ponty reflected on perceptual experience as enacted by the living body—or as he often stressed, by my body, which is the field of perception and action—he could not accept the traditional distinction made in classical psychology and philosophy between conceptions, as giving the form, and sensations, as giving the matter, in the constitution of knowledge. The consideration of perception in its whole setting, that is, in the "life-world," obviates the reduction of experience to what is judged to be true, to the simple sensory event, the *percipi*. Perceptions, as enacted, are already pregnant with *sens*; they are already a synthesis of concept and sensation, replete with meaning and direction. Or better, only an ideal analysis can abstract the pure sensation from its involvement with its *sens* in the living act of perception.

There is no question then of an epistemological priority regarding sensations and conceptions. Kant made us acknowledge that either of these apart from the other is bootless, one being "blind," the other "empty."[29] In Merleau-Ponty's paraphrase of Kant, "we can only think the world because we have already experienced it."[30] Thus when he attributes priority to perception, he is not reducing human knowledge to sensation; rather he is calling attention to the perceptual experience that is "our presence at the moment when things, truths, values are constituted for us."[31] It is this nonreflected experience, this act of the living body, by which we are anchored in the world given as actual and which "summons us to the tasks of knowledge and action."[32] The proper epistemological task of reflection is not to decompose this experience into its abstract components, which would be to deprive them of their meaning and their direction; it is rather to assist at this "birth of knowledge" by articulating the unified structure of living perception.

In this regard, Merleau-Ponty's investigation takes its point of departure from the distinction between "perceptual consciousness" and "intellectual consciousness." Here the epistemological priority is clear, even while the greater degree of clarity may belong to the latter. The intellectual act is characterized by an "active synthesis"; it grasps its object in the ideal clarity of a penetrating transparency. A cube, for example, is conceived with no foreshortening and no hidden sides; all its faces are equal and equally evident. In categorial thought, apart from perceptual consciousness, the object is grasped from everywhere at once, and this means that it is grasped from no point of view. It is not perceived at all, but merely conceived. And in this it is given either as possible or as necessary.

Perceptual consciousness, on the other hand, grasps its object in the modality of actuality. As enacted by the living body, perception has a place; it takes up a point of view and its world is given perspectivally. As a result, some aspects of the object are hidden, and others are "distorted." The perceived object is opaque and escapes full exposure to an ideal transparency. These "defects" are, Merleau-Ponty says, "the price of its being 'real'."[33] Indeed, they are the emblem of its actuality. Given in each of an indefinite series of perspectival views, but given exhaustively in no one of them, an actual object perpetually runs off into a horizon of further perceptions, so that a synthesis is required also to constitute the unity of the perceived object. But this synthesis is not an act of the intellectual order. Merleau-Ponty describes it as a "transition-synthesis," or a "horizonal synthesis," because in it perceptions enacted in differing moments, or from differing points of view, are united. The locus of this unity, however, is the living body in its habitual drawing together of its experiences into a concordant whole that constitutes its hold on its situation.

In this way Merleau-Ponty places the initial meaning-giving acts, Husserl's *Sinngebung*, on the level of perceptual consciousness, a stratum of experience that belongs to the engaged body and underlies intellectual consciousness, itself the locus of purely conceptual thought taken as a function of a conceivably disengaged "mind." The medium of expression appropriate to this primary stratum must itself be sensuous, that is, perceptible.

From this perspective the doubts created in Cézanne's mind might be thought of as stemming precisely from the tensions felt within the structure of his body at the peculiar differences between his actual perceptions of the reality of Nature—in Mont Sainte-Victoire serving as his subject—

and the reality of his painting in which he was trying to record his reading of the book of Nature. If Cézanne remained dissatisfied by his resolution of these tensions, Merleau-Ponty's analysis of perceptual consciousness helps locate the disparity that troubled the painter in the paradoxical nature of human openness onto the actual world, and it enables us to understand Cézanne's uncertainty as inherent to the phenomenon of authentic expression. This purpose of the painter—to interpret his own world in terms of his openness to it—is the context within which we may see where and why the slippage that created his persistent doubt occurred.

Considered as a problem of expression, it is evident that Cézanne was not confronted by the task of getting back into the world, as Galileo was owing to the scientist's preference for the medium of an ideal, conceptual language. The painter forged his interpretation directly in a perceptual medium—in what Merleau-Ponty would call "primary expression," because it arises from and speaks immediately to perceptual consciousness. In his paintings Cézanne could present for our personal experience, as well as for his own, an act of perceiving spatial relations whereby our cognition of space is grounded in the lived world. As a result, the need is obviated for any "translation" from "secondary expression," formulated through concepts with which intellectual consciousness deals, to the perceptual grasp of objects and the world presented in the mode of actuality.

Because his expression remained within the realm of perception, the slippage that led to his doubt was not that which may occur between thought and sensation. Indeed, as Merleau-Ponty notes, Cézanne rejected the ready-made dichotomies offered by tradition between sensation and judgment, between the painter who sees and the painter who thinks. He stressed the necessity for a "logical vision" and declared his aim to make nature and art the same. The source of his doubt must be sought in perceptual consciousness itself, and in the structure of primary expression. The world represented in a painting by Cézanne is the visual world of lived spatial relationships; in the paradoxical nature of this stratum of experience we may find a basis for explaining why Cézanne's stated aims were impossible to achieve.

Reflection on the act of perception, specifically on the experience of seeing, reveals that it is already a structure of consciousness—in Husserl's term, it is a manner of "intending" what is seen; as such it is already primary expression—what is seen gives itself within the horizon of visibility. In its structural unity, the phenomenon of seeing involves at once and with equal originality the act of seeing from a place, the visible object, and that object's being seen. But it also involves, just as essentially, the unseen. Given perspectivally, the perceived object hides those of its aspects that would be exposed to a different point of view, as well as that part of the landscape lying behind it; but also, to the extent that it commands focal attention, the seen object draws vision away from the horizon of the surrounding world, even though it cannot appear apart from this field of the vaguely seen, which marks the transition into the unseen.

In describing this basic fact of perspectival perception, Merleau-Ponty writes:

> No thing, no side of a thing, shows itself except by actively hiding the others, announcing them in the act of concealing them. To see is a matter of principle to see farther than one sees, to reach a latent existence. The invisible is the outline and depth of the visible. The visible does not admit of pure positivity any more than the invisible does.[34]

The visible perpetually slips off into the invisible; no actual perception escapes this paradox.

Precisely this opaqueness of the object and the "excessiveness" of the perceptible world, that is, their giving themselves to vision while always withholding something more, mark the object and the world as transcendent to the act of perception. But because these are what vision opens onto, the act of seeing is itself a transcendence: it reaches out beyond itself and makes known to itself something that is not sight itself. As such, vision opens onto a horizon of visibility, indeed of perceptibility, within which something more always remains to be seen, indeed to be perceived in all sensory modes. Something unseen is always intimated by the seen.

This paradox of appearing and hiding, of giving itself while always holding something back—another emblem of actuality—sets a problem for the body to solve. The self-imposed unity of any single solution is attained only at the cost of excluding other equally valid solutions, and therefore it remains "incomplete" with respect to the entire horizon of visibility. Neither a single object, nor much less the whole perceptible world, can be taken in fully by any one perception. Something is always left over.

In his "studies" Cézanne remained true to this characteristic structure of the phenomenon of perception. His *Mont Sainte-Victorie,* for example, shows us that more remains to be seen. The regions lying in peripheral vision offer other areas that could have been brought into focus, and the gradual transition into the unseen makes clear that the current field of vision could have been shifted. Cézanne reported his awareness of these endless possibilities when he wrote to his son that before a single subject he "could occupy [himself] for months without changing place, by turning now more to the right, now more to the left."[35] Expression, like perception itself, requires selection.

The painter is faced with the same choice as any perceiver: in order to see at all, a point of view must be taken up, a direction established, and some focal region chosen, each to the exclusion of other possibilities. His solution to the problem of expression brings forth one solution to the problem set by the perceptible world for the perceiving body. In the particularly felicitous solution achieved in this painting, Cézanne captured the sense of making a choice within the temporal flow of the act of perceiving by which the living body is continually engaged in its world.

Yet his expression, "fixed" as it is, does not reduce the solution to a timeless point-instant, as does a geometric conception. Rather it presents a moment of perception in which a space is opened up uniting far and near in a tense temporal spanning. Not only does the act of seeing, presented in his interpretation, reside within a series of earlier and later possible sights, but that act itself is stretched across a temporal span in which vision remains dynamically active, and in which alone perception lives. The spatial tension, established by the competing calls of the distant mountain and the near farmstead within the encircling indefinite distances revealed in peripheral vision, governs a moment of our own temporality and brings us to feel the "transition-synthesis" as it occurs in a moment of personal experience. The tense temporal spanning of this moment, during which a space is thrown open and brought to significance as our current perceptual situation, is the expressiveness of Cézanne's *Mont Sainte-Victoire.*

"Expressing what *exists* is an endless task," Merleau-Ponty wrote.[36] And so it is, precisely because the actual world perpetually slips away from perception. By showing themselves "in the imperious unity, the presence, the insurpassable plenitude which is for us the definition of the real,"[37] objects and the world run before perception and push its horizons, both spatial and temporal, further into the distance. This is the reason that objects of perception, as Husserl observed, always show themselves as already having been there when we first uncover them.[38] Likewise, it is the characteristic of perception by which we are given the experience of being in the world.

And yet, when Cézanne turned away from his primary mode of expression, from the brushes and pigments that compelled him to think in purely visual terms, and turned instead to the medium of language, where his thinking became "conceptual," he expressed the desire to recapture the whole of his motif; he said he wanted to present his mountain in its "full reality." But when he was unable to do so, to the satisfaction of these intellectual standards, he began to doubt his own ability as a painter. In one letter he even expressed the fear that he might be afflicted with a visual defect, similar to that attributed to El Greco. It seems obvious that, in his theoretical understanding and linguistic expression of this goal, he was thinking of the kind of "completeness" that is claimed for purely intellectual consciousness, and of the "strict reality" intended in scientific discourse. If this is the case, his own secondary expression, with its inherited vocabulary and sedimented concepts, and its projective idealizations, misled him into adopting an impossible standard. For as Merleau-Ponty's analysis makes clear, the very characteristics of perceptual experience that mark its object as actual must be abandoned when the aim is ideal completeness and absolute conceptual clarity.

We can only be thankful that the despair that emerged in Cézanne's writing and talking did not prevent him from painting. For there he bravely confronted the paradox of creative expression and, despite the intellectual doubts, produced works that give us to see, as if for the first time, the actual world coming into view even while it perpetually slips away.

However discomfited categorial thought may be by this slippage, perceptual thought becomes the transcendence that it is through spanning the openness between here, where we are placed whenever we see, and there, where our world stretches out before us; between what is present at a distance and what continually slips away. The genius of Cézanne's reading of the book of Nature resides in his having made this tension visible, and, in our reactions to his painting, felt within the structures of our "corporeal" being.

CHAPTER 6

Significance and Worldhood in Cézanne's Doubt

Cézanne's doubt stemmed from the same source as did Galileo's "failure" to conceptualize Nature as it presents itself to us: the ultimate reliance upon a secondary expression to convey a conceptually clearer idea of spatial reality than is attainable by an originary, and indeed intuitive, act of simply seeing. This, I have been maintaining, inverts the order of expression already announced in the dictum of Nietzsche, and more lately exposited by Merleau-Ponty. What is *gedacht,* concepts, clearly defined thought, can not precede an originary, creative expression, that is, an intuition of significance that can be realized only in execution. *Dichtung, poesis,* authentic expression, whereby a meaning horizon exhibiting its own norm is initially established, will always be presupposed by any secondary expression.

Without a clear account of such first-order, genuinely creative acts of expression in their capacity to make new meanings and new meaning horizons communally accessible, any effort to ground historical-social enterprises such as philosophy of natural science, including the sciences of language and indeed all epistemological inquiry, will forever be confronted by the antinomies that inevitably result from taking secondary expressions, the *gedacht,* as the basic phenomenon to be treated in the analysis of human understanding. Merleau-Ponty suggested as much in his admonishment that if we want to understand clearly the privileged position accorded to Reason, "we must begin by putting thought back among the phenomena of [authentic] expression."[1]

The question arises, then, how human beings experience the primary significances of their world and how these significances become expressed for others. In view of this question, the case of Cézanne's dilemma, in which he was caught between two modes of expression that conveyed incompatible interpretations of spatial reality, may be made to yield further "eidetic insights."

The credit belongs to Husserl for identifying the "life-world" as the locus of the "birth of knowledge" and for restoring it to the ranks of fundamental philosophical topics. Along with his contribution to methodology, his achievement was to establish our primordial awareness of this horizon as the point of return required by a philosophy that would fulfill its obligation to ground the concepts effective in cultural life and in human consciousness. Yet it is now clear that his decision to take the scientific reading of the book of Nature for his exemplum, for example, in the *Crisis,*[2] determined that his own investigation would not reach the primary experience of the life-world. Despite the immense importance of his sighting of this horizon, his focus on the origin of geometry and on Galileo's conception of a mathematized physical nature[3] deflected his last effort to elucidate the foundations of human understanding away from our worlds and into an analysis of secondary modes of expression. In similiar fashion, Cézanne's implicit adoption of a Galilean conception of "strict reality" deflected his efforts to say what he had accomplished on his canvases.

However influential mathematical language may have been during the past three centuries, and continues to be in our day, and however much the twentieth-century crisis in the sciences demanded a new effort to ground them in the life-world, Husserl's analysis of scientific expression inevitably brought him to the impasse of a *cogito* intending an ideal conceptual model. We need only remember that Descartes's *cogito* argument has been replaced in Husserl's writings by the transcendental reduction, which yields as a residue of analysis a transcendental ego.

Reflection on secondary expression can go back only as far as "intellectual consciousness." Even when the "transcendental ego" is described as a transcendence, as always a "consciousness of" something other than itself, the problem of accounting for the actuality (or "objectivity") of what this "pure subjectivity" opens onto remains.

Merleau-Ponty's redirection of phenomenological description, by which primary expression was made the basic exemplum to be examined, placed the emphasis on a genuinely corporeal *cogito.* For him, the last stand of phenomenological reduction was to the grounding relationship between a living body and its world. As early as his first major work, *The Structure of Behavior*,[4] Merleau-Ponty had maintained that the relation between mind and body can only be expressed in correlative terms. In his description of the ultimate continuity between the orders of forms—syncretic, mutable, and symbolic—each is accounted for as a different kind of patterning of behavior in the life of human subjects. Within the "dialectic of orders," from the physical to the vital and thence to the cultural, presumably completed only by the human species of organism, each lower order of the dialectic constitutes "body" for the immediately higher order of conduct, which is its "mind."[5]

This transformation of Husserlian phenomenology was further elaborated in *Phenomenology of Perception*, where the "birth of knowledge" was situated in perceptual consciousness. The "subject" that achieves knowledge is no longer thought of, à la Husserl, as "a constituting consciousness and, as it were, a pure being-for-itself"; but neither is it the objective body as conceived in physiology, "a chemical structure or an agglomeration of tissues."[6] Rather, this "subject, which takes a point of view, is my body as the field of perception and action"; or, as Merleau-Ponty often stresses, it is the body that I am, the lived body, which is my "general medium for having a world."[7] Beginning with a focus on this corporeal subject Merleau-Ponty develops the central thesis of his *Phenomenology*—the primacy of perception—by drawing out the philosophical consequences of recognizing that the relations and the type of organization belonging to the perceived world are not reached through deductions performed by a pure intellect. Research by Gestalt psychologists had shown that a significant structure remains in the perceptually experienced world even when the intellect has been severely impaired. Such organization, and in particular the quality of the perceived as "real," cannot be accounted for if subject and object, mind and body, are initially separated. For Merleau-Ponty, what is primary is a *corps-sujet*, an embodied subject, whose acts of perception amount to a nonreflected engagement in its actual world. The ego of intellectual consciousness is certain of its own existence, as well as the world's "objectivity," by virtue of an organic tie: both intellection and perception are modes of behavior performed by the same conscious body.

This corporeal *cogito*, then, replaces both Descartes's and Husserl's interpretations of the thinking, knowing ego. In reflection it recaptures itself in act, already engaged in the horizon of its operations where it has already taken up a point of view and established a direction. It experiences the significances of its world from the particular perspective of the body that enacts perceptual consciousness. As engaged, and as nonreflective, this act opens onto a transcendent world by which the subject is affected in its unitary being. The fact that its experiences form a concordant whole is not guaranteed, as it would be for a "universal thinker," such as the phenomenologist's transcendental ego; rather, this fact is merely contingent and is always "menaced."[8]

By focusing on the birth of knowledge as it occurs in the experience of an embodied consciousness, Merleau-Ponty brought phenomenological description to bear on the experiences of primary significance as something that is to be continually enacted, and on their expressions as patterns of behavior that are performed in historical moments within a cultural milieu. On this basis, he sought to clarify the structure of human existence whereby it has "a preobjective view" of its world—the structure he called *l'être-au-monde,* "being-toward-the-world."[9]

This emphasis on the primacy of perception led Merleau-Ponty to reflect on the achievements of his countryman whose paintings allow us to experience the life-world, insofar as the painter had made it visible, at the level of corporeal existence. We have found that Cézanne focused on this stratum of experience whenever he was able to "forget" what he had been taught and held himself open instead to what was presented in innocent, unsophisticated perceptual experience as he looked out on his world and was captivated by the wondrous, wordless expanse lying before his eyes and revealing a significance that he could express only through a harmonious organization of colors.

Reflecting on this preobjective mode of experience, Merleau-Ponty sought to elucidate the act of perception whereby the spatiality of the life-world is grasped before being reflected upon. He recognized that the results of Cézanne's efforts interpreted the experienced space of the world in a direct manner such as could only be dreamed of by Galileo as somehow correlated with mathematical formulations. With this focus on perception as a genuinely corporeal understanding, Merleau-Ponty secured the contact of his reflection with "present and living reality," just as it is experienced by a conscious body.

The question, then, of how human beings experience and express the primary significances of their worlds becomes centered on the comportment of historical, embodied "subjects" engaged in living their existence within the open horizon of a meaningful situation.

When the transcendental reduction was replaced in Merleau-Ponty's modification of the phenomenological method, the correlation between a *corps-sujet*, or conscious body, and the perceived world became the grounding relationship for his reflection. But it is clear that this fundamental correlation remains centered on existent entities; reflection is still directed to entities as such, either as perceived or as perceiving. Hence, the results will remain ontic.

Although Merleau-Ponty's description identifies the essential structure whereby a living body must always be situated in a world, his characteristic concern for entities—either a perceiver or a perceived—prevents him from accounting for the a priori unity of this structure. The totality of the horizonal structure is said to result from a "transition-synthesis," or a "horizonal synthesis," albeit performed at the level of corporeal existence. Yet, as noted earlier in connection with Husserl's account of the synthesis of the life-world,[10] a synthetic unity, even when "passively constituted," always arrives too late to serve its required function as context for a "first" perception.

Although Merleau-Ponty acknowledges the unity of perceptual experience in his stress on "global perception," and the unity of the perceived world in his noting of its "global configuration," that is, its gestalt, the single structure in which these two unities themselves are already correlated remains unclarified. Specifically, the act of perceiving, as opposed to the perceiver and the perceived, is not thematically elucidated in its difference from the entity that performs it, even though this act is implicit in his description of the unitary phenomenon exhibiting these three structural moments.

The function of perceiving in the lives of human subjects is indeed made clear in Merleau-Ponty's phenomenology of perception, but its origin in their existential structures is not. The reason for this omission seems obvious: perceiving, as a manner of comportment, is not itself an entity but is instead a way of being that belongs to an entity that perceives; its analysis, then, will be ontological.

The writings from Merleau-Ponty's last years indicate that he was working his way toward a method of ontological analysis.[11] They also show that he had not yet gained command of the required interpretive tools when his career was brought to its untimely end. Anyone who has attempted to lay out the metaphors on which "Eye and Mind" depends will be aware of the lack of clear ontological *explicata* in this last rumination on the dilemma posed by Cézanne's doubt. Indeed, Merleau-Ponty alerts his reader to the projective character of this essay:

> Yet this philosophy still to be done is that which animates the painter . . . when, in Cézanne's words, he "thinks in painting."[12]

The means for analyzing the act, as opposed to entities, still eluded him. For this reason, in his most thoroughly realized works the phenomenological method, though now clearly existential, yields merely ontic results—even as it did in Husserl's "transcendental" descriptions.[13]

In this regard Heidegger may be seen to have offered us a means for revising both Husserl and Merleau-Ponty: Husserl by replacing descripton with a hermeneutical ontology, and Merleau-Ponty by showing the existential structures implicit in the Frenchman's ontic results. The "development" traced here is, of course, anachronistic if one respects the strict chronology of published texts. Yet in light of the respective contributions to the phenomenological tradition made by these three towering figures, the direction taken by

Merleau-Ponty's own thought—from a distinctly Husserlian beginning to the Heideggerian interests evidenced by the last works—gives credibility to this reading of the development of phenomenology as "universal science."

Husserl identified the required horizon and called it the life-world; Merleau-Ponty explained that it could be reached in its actuality only by a *cogito* that is genuinely corporeal; and Heidegger showed how any ontic point of departure—in particular as the "corporeal *cogito*" of Merleau-Ponty or the phenomenological reduction to and description of the "transcendental ego" of Husserl—has to eventuate in an ontological understanding and interpretation of the structures implicit in the basic condition of human existence: Being-in-the-world.

Corresponding to the corporeal *cogito* of Merleau-Ponty is the "a priori existential"[14] of a human being's spatiality. Even if perception is a privileged means of access to the real world of science or Nature, it is a mode of conduct made possible by a human existent's habit of living in its own worlding (read "significant") world. Hence, corresponding to our ontic reading of Cézanne's painting given previously, we must be able to construct an ontological reading of Cézanne's act of spatializing his own felt spatiality.

We move, then, from Merleau-Ponty's philosophical anthropology to Heidegger's fundamental ontology, that is, his interpretation of the existential structures of human being, for the means to interpret the comportment in which primary significances are experienced and expressed so as to establish the meaningful situation shared by all who participate with us in cultural life. Cézanne's primary, and Galileo's secondary, readings of the book of Nature may be retained as our principal examples of expressive comportment. And the dilemma posed by Cézanne's doubt, which arose from his inability to comprehend the tension between these two modes of expression, remains the exemplary problem to be resolved.

On Heidegger's perspective, the task of the ontologist is to find the words by which to make explicit the understanding of our own being that we already have by virtue of our familiarity with it—an understanding, however suppressed it may be, that grounds the projections of our being and is always presupposed by our significant dealings with our world. Fortunately, at this assignment Heidegger was as much the master of his medium as Cézanne was of his, despite the carping of critics who are unwilling to confront creative expression in philosophical discourse. Unfortunately, however, for purposes of our exposition, many of the words Heidegger found in the available vocabulary had to be wrenched free from their familiar meanings and compelled to convey new meanings. His task was to elucidate precisely those structures of human existence that everyday language, and indeed the history of ontology on his view, tend to obscure.

The creative philosopher, like the creative painter, can use only what is available in his historical situation, but when familiar terms with their sedimented meanings will not serve, the old terms must be used in unconventional ways and made to discriminate just what conventional language does not. When he succeeds, the new meanings will emerge within the meaning horizon established by the structure of his discourse; norms for interpreting an expression still lie in its structure, whether that expression is couched in Heidegger's philosophical discourse or presented to vision by Cézanne's harmonious organization of colors. In either case, the same spirit of cooperation, the same willingness to entertain the proffered meanings in their setting, is required of anyone who would not simply reject them out of hand. And in its turn, a brief exposition of Heidegger's achievement must call for a similar indulgence when a technical term or a strange-sounding phrase must be used because no accurate substitute is readily available. We need only recall that we are describing structures of human existence, moments constitutive of human being; for this purpose, the language of "substance" and of strictly ontic analysis clearly would be misleading, if not entirely inappropriate.

When we do read Cézanne on his own doubts and Heidegger on the structures of human experience, it becomes relatively easy to see how the latter's ontological characterizations are relevant to an aesthetic inquiry into creation as a modification of meanings within an already established meaning horizon. In the philosopher's language we may find a way of saying what the painter could not say in his own words, namely how he found himself attuned to nature, with an understanding that he could bring to clear expression in the primary medium of painting, but not in his secondary medium of language. For this purpose we turn to Heidegger's analysis of how a human being is in the world.

In Heidegger's account of the matter at issue, the basic state of human existence, being-in-the-world, is a unitary phenomenon.[15] In whatever mode it may have been concretized by actual human comportment, whether in acts of perception, conception, or other expressive behavior, the whole of this structure is implicated as the condition for the possibility of any significant patterning of behavior. As the structure of our own being, it is familiar even though an understanding of it may be suppressed for the most part. Such a suppression would likely produce doubts in the most perceptive of painters, as it did in Cézanne.

Because it is a unitary phenomenon, the whole of being-in-the-world must be kept firmly in view. Nevertheless, an articulation of its structure may bring various components to the fore for emphasis. One component, "the-world" in the sense of "worldhood," has already been examined as the *existential* that underlies and makes possible the scientific conception of Nature as an objective physical world (Chapter 4). The consideration of Cézanne's primary expression and Merleau-Ponty's reflection on the painter's doubt has brought us to the place where "being-in" may be made to show itself as the implicate of all communication, but which is most clearly brought to view in acts of artistic creation. This *existential*, which characterizes the mode of comportment described as "dwelling in" or "inhabiting" a world, provides the ontological clue required for resolving the dilemma of Cézanne's doubt.

Dwelling in the world, or inhabiting a region, as opposed to merely occurring at a location within some previously designated space, indicates a manner of comportment in which one understandingly reckons with what is encountered in his vicinity. It manifests a basic familiarity with "closeness." (Heidegger's phrase is "*in der Nähe.*"[16]) Instruments and materials used in carrying on one's business exhibit varying degrees of closeness, experienced as qualitative differences. For example, an item of use is "hard to reach," or it is conveniently placed so as to be "handy."

In dealing with entities, we assign them a proper place in our vicinity, determined by the task at hand and measured by their own "resistance" to our aims. As such, "reckoning" expresses our own sense of residing in an open region, of having access to the world in its nearness and farness, whether or not concepts of homogeneous objective space and quantitative units of distance have yet been cognized. Indeed, this awareness of an opening constantly exuded round about oneself, in which entities are arranged, is the primary experience of the spatiality of our life-world. And it is this that makes possible the conceptualizing of geometrical space, even as Husserl intimated in his description of the origins of geometry in practical endeavors.

In this "sense" of my own locale, felt as a tension between here and there, I am aware of being directed toward my world that surrounds me on all sides. From the here where I am, the world lies off there in the direction from which entities come forth to meet me, and toward which I am summoned as the region of my possibilities. In the experience of this tension, here and there are qualitatively distinct though strictly correlative; the farness of things is conquered, though not obliterated, so that my region is felt to lie within my reach. It is brought near. Correlatively, I am stretched across the gap in which I experience myself as having room to move, and as capable of effecting changes in what lies there, and in this experience, I always find myself attuned, in some way or other, to what surrounds me. Heidegger notes that this primordial sense of spatiality is characterized by "de-distancing and directionality" (*Ent-fernung und Ausrichtung*).[17] It is a sense of aligning things in a significant order within a vicinity over which I exercise a certain dominion. According to Merleau-Ponty, that kind of control is the "knowledge" every human being possesses of its body. And on this basis, I "know" my actual placement in the real world as an ontic situation, felt as a tension in the intentional arc of my body's relating itself to the objects of its world.

This "knowledge," or felt significance, located by Merleau-Ponty at the level of "perceptual consciousness," is described by Heidegger as a structure of human existence and as ontologically more primordial than linguistic articulation. For either philosopher, this "understanding" belongs to a stratum of experience underlying concrete utterance in actual language or even silent formulation in a proposition. Thus it may be called prepropositional, or prelinguistic understanding. It is a grasping of significance that, as Heidegger says, has no need of speech; its expression takes the form of dealing with the situation at hand, and it is discernible even when such dealings also involve the use of speech as an appropriate tool.

When this "sense" is grounded in one's placement in his ontic situation so as to be genuinely his own, and not rather adopted from secondary expressions to be imposed on the situation, Heidegger calls it "disclosedness,"[18] because it is the structure by which the worldhood of a human's world is brought to show itself. This existential characterizes a human existent's primary openness to his world; it is the access given by virtue of being human. In *Being and Time* this structure is explicated under the heading of "The Existential Constitution of the 'There' "[19]—or of the *Da*, a significantly ambiguous German adverb meaning both "here" and "there."

In its unity, the structure of the *Da* exhibits three moments, together constituting the sense of being-in the world wherein one dwells. *Befindlichkeit*,[20] the condition of feeling the tension of the here-there, is the affectivity by which any human existent is always attuned to the qualitative whole of its region at any moment of its life. To this attunement belongs an understanding (*Verstehen*[21]), as well as an "expressivity" or "discourse" (*Rede*[22]). Thus, when Heidegger characterizes the basic condition of human existence as "Being-there," he indicates the full structure—usually given as a preontological comprehension of an inquirer's being—comprised of finding oneself disposed in some way toward the world, with a complementary feeling of being so disposed that is a necessary part of any ontological understanding that may be given full expression in the ontologist's linguistic utterance. These three moments, affectivity, understanding, and expression, are said to constitute a single structural complex; they spring from that same source, which is exemplified in every ontic situation.

Heidegger's interpretation of these three features belonging to the structure of disclosedness, as the unitary phenomenon of being-in the world, and as an essential condition of distinctively human existence, provides an ontological foundation for a general theory of aesthetics capable of explicitly laying out the case of Cézanne's creativity as well as its accompanying uncertainty.

To come to grips with Cézanne's act of spatial representation, it is of particular importance to see the import of Heidegger's characterization of understanding itself as "projection" (*Entwurf*[23]). On his ontological interpretation, any understanding pertains to a potentiality for being in the world, and as a structure of disclosedness, this potentiality belongs to the whole of being-in-the-world. In understanding, the possibilities for one's own being—qua understanding—are projected, and indeed precisely as possibilities for his being-in-the-world. Heidegger explicates this projective character of understanding when he describes what he calls its "fore-structure" (*Vor-struktur*[24]). Because what is understood is always "thrown" onto a horizon held in advance and brought forth into the "sight" of understanding already conceived in some way, this prospective mode of human existence consists of a fore-having, a fore-sight, and a fore-conception.[25] Any concretely realized interpretation, in which the possibilities of understanding are worked out, will operate on the basis of this fore-structure.

To follow Heidegger's development of a "fundamental ontology," we begin with what we all have before us; it is the totality of involvements—the worldhood of our worlds—experienced as a felt significance. Without possessing this basis of an interpretation we simply have nothing to which to apply his distinctions. Fore-having is therefore a mode of being toward this structural whole, and we live this relationship understandingly; at first, however, the significance of the subject's world is felt—as a mood.

Out of this whole, something is selected by foresight; a "cut" is made in the whole and some articulable entity is made to stand out for specific attention, even if it is only a mountain at a distance.

But as made conspicuous, and brought into focal awareness, this entity is already conceived in some manner; this manner has been decided in advance by the fore-conception, for example, as being far away and as focal point for our encroaching vision. Because anything understood is always understood "as" something lying within the context of a particular regard, this "as" is called hermeneutical and indicates the horizon in which an interpretation may operate.[26]

Together, these aspects of a preliminary understanding

constitute the existential ground on which any interpretation will ultimately rely, if it is indeed to bring into view what it talks about, and if it is to make explicit what is sighted in an original openness to its topic. Fundamentally, it is the prior felt significance that constitutes that onto which all understanding is projected, so that all meaning, all intelligibility, all signification presupposes this characterization of being-in-the-world. Any factical, that is, historically actualized, understanding has "always already" understood this horizon, which is the ultimate foundational "meaning horizon" for any communicative act. When a painter attempts to realize in a painting the way distant objects are brought near he must base himself on an understanding he already possesses of his own spatial existence, even if that understanding cannot be brought to verbal clarity. His work attempts to show how that spatiality looks!

Briefly, what this means for a general aesthetic theory is that an "aesthetic object," a work of art, such as a painting, novel, poem, sculpture, or symphony, will be encountered in the world, but "cut" out of that totality through a procedure such as phenomenological "bracketing" and conceived in its manner of being as a "work"—whereupon the art work itself will be revealed as a "world," or context of significance, within which its identifiable counters may be fore-sighted and conceived in their structural relatedness as presenting a unique significance, which may be termed the expressiveness of the work.

This expressiveness will have been understood when the tensions felt to subsist among its various counters have been resolved, in one's experience of them, as they fund into a single significance, that is, as they all work together.

Having experienced this expressiveness, one may take up the critic's task of finding the words to make explicit, in a second-level expression, what and how the first-order expression was seen to be. This interpretive task, then, is analogous to that of the ontologist, or of the metaphysician; but the aesthetic critic has the surety that comes from knowing that the "world" he seeks to explicate *is* only to the extent that it is expressed by the work lying open before him, even as it lies open to his fellow observers.

And to the extent that the artistic expression *works* in the lives of other people, it stands as an autonomous base for the mutual understanding that is required by any act of communication.

On Heidegger's phenomenological-ontological interpretation of human disclosedness, applied to the realm of aesthetic appreciation, a doctrine of communication emerges whereby creative expression is seen to be fundamental to the establishment of a mutual understanding on which all communication depends. The ultimate "meaning horizon," as I have been using this term, is furnished by a human being's prior understanding of its relationship to a world. This is the phenomenon Heidegger referred to as the worldhood of the world. It is such an understanding that comes to expression in works of art.

For this reason, any investigation into the foundations of human understanding must eventually confront the subject matter of aesthetic inquiry. For it is in acts of artistic expression, of *dichten*, that the prior understanding of being-in-the-world is first brought to expression in originary contexts of significance capable of "working" independently of other expressions. In such works, the full circle of concretely interpreting the prior understanding that belongs to one's being-there, that is, to being in the same world that is disclosed by the very act of expression, is brought to realization in an expressive object that may gain the required independence from the historical context of its execution in the life of the artist so as to exhibit its own significance for appreciation in the lives of others. In aesthetic expressions, the horizon of authentic understanding, merely presupposed by secondary expressions, is brought to stand in the structure of the work itself; through such independently significant artifacts, a multiplicity of human existents may come to recognize themselves as mutually being-toward a single "world" and thus as being-with one another.

In a painting by Cézanne, for example, his *Mont Sainte-Victoire*, it is clear that what we find is not a representation of "real," that is, scientific, space. On that conception (fore-conception) of his achievement, his work would indeed be three steps removed from reality: it would express his understanding of the geometer's conception of a Platonic ideal reality. But the reversal indicated by Nietzsche's dictum, and its development within the phenomenological tradition, have led us to turn aright—or, better, to twist free of—the inverted world of Platonism. As a result, we shall see first, understandingly to be sure, and interpret perceptual experience for what it is in our ownmost experience: the comportment by which the spatiality of our own worlding world is disclosed. And Cézanne's painting will be seen as the record of his act of spatializing his world, that is, of bestowing an alignment upon perceived entities and giving them a place in his own region. His painting will present an interpretation executed in a medium that allows its viewers to have the primary experience by which a visible world is initially disclosed. Hence this will be a public, or intersubjective, world in that his painting reveals a vicinity that is shared with others, insofar as anyone can also take up the point of view established by the painting.

Merleau-Ponty, for one, has criticized the traditional reading of what the painter represents. Specifically, he has shown that Cézanne's act of painting is not a secondary expression treating of conceived space, as many Renaissance paintings actually were. Rather it is a primary expression, arising out of and presenting to experience the act of "seeing" space. This act, interpreted in the *Mont Sainte-Victoire*, is made our own when we allow it to become the object of our perception. On this corporeal foundation, the perceived landscape is experienced as "present and living reality," and the work of the creative artist shows how it is that we are open to this mountain, seen in this light from a perch above a farm across the plain. His interpretation, concretely expressed, strikes closer to the bone than does the scientist's mathematical formulation, which speaks from a general point of view separated through abstraction from the living reality it would interpret. As a result of this removal to a general "perspective," a scientific-mathematical interpretation requires some means for returning from its conceptual constructions and getting back into the texture of our own real world. But Cézanne presents this world, in its qualitative richness, to a personally lived perspective.

Heidegger, however, has shown that even "primary expressions" are still ontic, taking place in space and time. As such, they are made possible by a prior understanding of the significance of one's being-in-a-world. But when an artist, like Cézanne, launches his work from the foundation of this structure of his own existence, from his ownmost openness to his world, he may bring to expression in his ontic act an interpretation of what is familiar to him by virtue of his own disclosedness. His ontic acts are guided by his ontological understanding, even when he is unable to bring this understanding to fruition by any means other than that of organizing colors, and if, as in Cézanne's case, he never finds the words to make clear what is so evident to his eye and hand. In his act of painting, he "realizes" one possibility projected in his own understanding of being-in his world. Specifically, Cézanne makes visible the spatiality of his world through that act which is inseparably an experiencing and an expressing of its primary perceptual significance. In this act he spatializes his world, and he does so in a mode of comportment that concretely works out his prior understanding, so that others also may experience what he has understood.

An ontologist, such as Heidegger, lays out his interpretation in the medium of philosophical discourse, but a painter, such as Cézanne, "thinks in painting," and his interpretation is couched in the primary medium of organized colors. His expression, then, speaks more directly than even the philosopher's, as Heidegger himself has acknowledged by attributing the primary role in the originary establishment of contexts of significance to the activity of creative artists.[27]

When Cézanne, or anyone else, "thinks in painting" a fore-conception of spatiality is the specific prior understanding of significance that grounds and guides his efforts to "realize" an interpretation in an act of concrete expression. And this projected significance will be fulfilled when it has been made visible in the structures of his painting. It is this anticipated end that will allow him to judge that his act of expression has come to completion—a judgment he must make from the same perceptual standpoint anyone else may take up. In an aesthetic expression, the only relevant norm is found in the work itself.

Cézanne's *Mont Sainte-Victoire*, for example, establishes a unique *here* toward which the whole landscape is made to flee by the painter's organization of colors. When the chaos of color "sensations" coalesces into a single significance, the percipient is *placed* with relation to the *there* of the represented landscape. The alignment given to the mountain, the plain, and the farmstead determines a "culminating point" that is the apex of the "cone" projected by perspectival vision. The resolution of the tension between precisely these far and near perceptual objects takes place only when this specific point of view has been taken up, in a moment of cooperation with the painter. This uniquely defined perspective looks down on the farm buildings, across the indeterminate plain, and toward the distant mountain rising above eye level and into the clouded sky. Indeed, the distinctiveness of this act of vision extends to the areas of focus: predominantly the distant mountain, with the nearer farm competing for focal attention. As the indefinite plain lying between these spreads into peripheral vision, it shows that the chosen perspective lies in a field of other possibilities. In realizing this qualitatively particularized view, the painting concretely establishes the directionality that in general characterizes all disclosures of spatiality.

Likewise, it concretely expresses the "bringing close," or "de-distancing," that belongs to such disclosing. In that moment of cooperation when this painting is allowed to work, when one takes up the here uniquely determined by the there opened up in the painting, the landscape is brought into one's vicinity. Indeed, for the moment, it is one's vicinity; the far mountain and the near farmstead are brought into "contact" with the surface of the current visual field. In that moment the distance severing here and there is overcome by vision as it follows the directions given by Cézanne's gesture. Experienced as brought into reach, the landscape becomes the region in which one dwells. And because the painter's gesture is available to anyone who will see, this region is accessible to others; this painting allows an experience of a mutual being-toward that amounts to the communion with others Heidegger called "Being-with" (*Mit-Sein*[28]).

Cézanne's interpretation of this segment of his world, of this moment in his history, exhibits the structures of his own disclosedness, that is, his manner of being open to the world before him. Having the experience of the tension between his current here and there, and understanding that experience as a moment of his own being-in-the-world, he had already conceived his visible situation in terms of his "fore-conceived" spatiality. His projection of this understanding toward the possibilities of interpretation came to be worked out ontically, through the unity of his eye and hand, in the act of manipulating colors so as to record the ontological act of spatializing in which the genuinely real world of the painter is brought to explicit understanding. His act of creative expression, then, is inseparably ontic and ontological. It is an act of dealing with entities in space and time, guided by and expressive of the tacit understanding of his own being—an understanding he has by virtue of being open to the world where his possibilities lie.

Owing to his return to a primordial level of awareness of his world, from which he forged this expression, he achieved an interpretation of spatiality on the basis on an understanding underlying all secondary conceptions of space. That is, he showed how a "vicinity" comes to make its appearance in a primary experience. Hence, in an ontological interpretation of *Mont Sainte-Victorie*, we do not find a representation of space conceived as an isotropic, homogeneous field where objects may occupy a multiplicity of places. This painting does not represent Galilean space, as did those of the Renaissance painters with their science of vanishing points and geometrical "deep perspective." Cézanne has represented spatiality, which is experienced to be a fundamental dimension of the life-world and is understood a priori as the significance of the relational totality of the perceived world.

It is the creative act of spatializing, perceptually experienced and perceptually expressed, that satisfies the painter's persistent drive to "read Nature" in its own terms, yet not merely as a passive copyist. Painting is not mechanical.

> The man of letters expresses himself in abstractions whereas a painter, by means of drawing and colour, gives concrete form to his sensations and perceptions. One is neither too scrupulous nor too sincere nor too submissive to nature; but one is more or less master of one's model, and above all, of the means of expression.[29]

To give concrete form to sensations and perceptions is to manifest one's own "creativity."

Cézanne's "thinking in painting" could be concretely expressed only by the act of painting, and the results of those acts prove that he understood, in the primary manner that makes it possible for one to be a painter, the spatiality onto which an understanding of the visible world has already been projected. In his painting we find the structures of his world expressed through a spatialization of that significance. Thus, we are also brought to acknowledge that he "knew," though in a manner inseparable from the behavior proper to a painter, that there is ontological understanding only when it is "realized" in an interpretation that communicates. For the artist, this means performing the ontic act of making visible the structures of the world wherein he dwells. His ontological understanding must itself be brought to stand in an object accessible to others.

When he has achieved this "objectification," he has bequeathed to us all an artifact embodying an originary expression of a primary experience. Through the mediation of such works, that is, through their working in our attentive experience of them, communication takes place, and indeed on a primary level of our own essential openness to the world. On the basis of such "working works" (read "expressing" works) our own being-toward a world may come to be explicitly understood as a *mutual being-toward* in which a common meaning horizon is shared. Specifically, in the art of a painter such as Cézanne, spatiality is revealed as the significance of the perceived world, and it is this that is idealized into space by geometers and generalized into the concept of physical objects by physicists such as Galileo.

In sum, a criticism is an interpretation of a painting in the same way—that is, as implementing the same structures—as an act of painting is an interpretation of the painter's being-in-the-world. In each case the interpretation implicates the existential structures of affectivity, understanding, and discourse, which together constitute the disclosing of the "there." Both the critic and the painter find themselves attuned to the felt tensions of a context of significance selected from the range of their current totality of involvements. For a representational painter of nature such as

Cézanne, these are the perceptual tensions felt before his motif, or the experience of the vibrant push and pull of what he called "sensations of color." In his being-toward this segment of his perceived world, there already lies an understanding of the specific here-there that is fore-conceived in terms of spatiality, that is, in terms of directionality and de-distancing. Because he projects his own being onto the possibilities proper to a painter, he "thinks" this understanding in the medium of organized colors, and his "discourse" or *logos* issues forth in a painting. Enter the critic.

A critic exhibits the same existential structures, but he takes the artist's work for his context of significance and seeks the words to make explicit the expressiveness experienced in his own being-toward the "world" creatively established by the painter's act. Thus his interpretation expresses his prior understanding in which he fore-conceived the painting in terms of its "being a work," that is, as a complete expressive artifact setting up a "world" and making it visible. His own experience of the work in its structural unity, his experience of its significance, grounds his interpretation, and the anticipatory conception of its unique expressiveness is what he projects onto the possibility of an explicit criticism, which will issue forth in his own act of discourse.

In either case, significant expression is made possible by the existential structures of being-in-the-world; and when a possibility of interpreting one's own world has been realized, the painter or the critic will have revealed himself as a "disclosing being," and indeed authentically so to the extent that his projection of an interpretation has been resolutely worked out on the basis of his own openness to the significance of his world, so as to bring that significance to light in the structure of his own expressive gesture.

Cézanne exhibited his authentic disclosing of significance in his acts of primary expression, namely when he painted. Yet when he turned to what was for him a mode of secondary expression—language—and attempted to interpret verbally the conditions and aims of his art, it is evident that he had adopted a conceptual scheme inadequate to his own achievements as a painter. Heidegger's analysis of the fore-structure of understanding enables us to comprehend what went wrong, and to see that Cézanne's doubt emerged from the conflict between his own disclosing of his world and the inherited explanation of the "real" world conceived in Galilean science as objective physical nature. This scientific explanation may now be seen to be inadequate as an account of creative expression precisely because it is strictly ontic, and because it takes secondary expressions—conceptions belonging to intellectual consciousness—as the locus of the "true" picture of our world.

On a Galilean interpretation of the painter's art, the artist imitates the secondary qualities of physical objects, that is, their colors, in a point for point correspondence between his canvas, taken as a "window onto Nature," and a plane imagined as lying across his visual field perpendicular to his line of sight. What he "has in advance" while standing before his motif are the sensations caused by light falling on his retina from geometrically determinate directions. As a result of these sensations he can pick out an arrangement of physical objects constituting the landscape. These are conceived beforehand as the cause of the variations in light determined by their shape properties and their location in space at an objective distance and direction from the point in space occupied by his body. His painting, then, gives its viewers the illusion of occupying that same point. But the original conception of the space in which that point is located remains as mysterious as the mind of God.

On this interpretation the painter is merely a slow and awkward camera, devoted to copying what God's creation causes to appear in the painter's vision, indeed the image that falls on his retina. His own "creativity" is reduced to his taste in selecting scenes to portray, and to his skill in reproducing them convincingly. Descartes analyzed visual art in just this Galilean manner in his *Dioptric*, where he interpreted vision as something to be thought in accord with the laws of geometry. And the mathematical "vanishing-point perspective," made into a science of representing objects located in cubical space by Renaissance painters, continued to have such an influence on art theory that Cézanne's contemporaries attributed his "deformations" to simple ineptitude.

Although Merleau-Ponty's phenomenological analysis of perception dispenses with the causal theory of sensations and reunites the painter's thinking with his perceiving, his interpretation remains ontic. Because he was unsuccessful in making the turn from entities to their being, the dilemma of Cézanne's doubt still perplexed him to the end of his career. The reason for this failure now seems obvious: in his analysis space continues to be the fore-conception that guides the painter. Despite this, Merleau-Ponty came very close to an adequate solution with his doctrine of the unity found in a preobjective perceptual consciousness.

On this theory, what is held in the fore-having is the painter's perceptual situation, and this includes an awareness of his eye and hand coordination, with the possibilities for expression implied in that "knowledge" of his own body. What is fore-sighted is the landscape, composed of objects at a distance; yet it must be constituted in an act of "passive," that is, corporeal, synthesis that results in a global perception. The landscape, then, is fore-conceived in terms of space. But even for a perceptual consciousness, "space" can be derived only through an abstraction from the objective locations of entities placed in relation to one another, and this abstraction implies some even more fundamental understanding. Yet, because the "stratum" of preobjective experience serves in Merleau-Ponty's analysis as the locus of the "birth of knowledge" and as the ultimate foundation of primary expression, we would have no right to speak of a more fundamental understanding than what occurs in perceptual consciousness.

This difficulty exposes the inadequacy of taking entities as fundamental in human understanding, even when a correlation, for example, between an embodied subject and its world, is said to constitute this foundation. The act of correlating, or the manner of being in which a world is initially given in its significance, is implied as the genuinely original unity that Merleau-Ponty came so close to interpreting. Yet until the ontological turn is made, this manner of being must remain at best only implicit.

On the ontological interpretation of Cézanne's act of creative expression, which I have offered in the perhaps unsettling vocabulary of Heidegger's hermeneutical ontology, it is clear that as a painter Cézanne brought to fruition in his *Mont Sainte-Victoire* the structure of his own disclosedness Heidegger called *Rede*. What he expressed was his prior understanding (*Verstehen*) that accompanies his affectivity (*Befindlichkeit*).

In the fore-structure of this understanding, what Cézanne had in advance was his own being-in-the-world. And his foresight had cut out of this totality the qualitatively distinct tension perceptually felt between the here and there as he stood on the hill above Les Lauves and looked across the plain toward Mont Sainte-Victoire. Directed toward this segment of his world as an open region affecting him from afar, he had fore-conceived it in terms of his own spatiality—the structure of his existence by which he disclosed a vicinity and aligned entities through his own act of spatializing. His task, then, as a painter was to interpret this significance in an act of expression whereby it would become clear to him and accessible to any others who would cooperate with his gesture by turning their own being toward the phenomenal context that is his painting.

The painter's task has been completed when his prior understanding, indeed this moment in his own disclosing of his worlding world, becomes visible in the structure of his painting. And the critic's task is fulfilled when his own expression has made explicit the significance experienced in the face of what the artist has wrought.

What then is the significance of Cézanne's doubt? This dilemma that so perplexed Merleau-Ponty is resolved in an ontological interpretation when it is seen that the worldhood of Cézanne's life was disclosed through two modes of expression, and his exercise of these resulted in conflicting interpretations of Nature's reality. As a painter he relied on his own openness to the world, and he succeeded in authentically expressing the significance revealed through his own existence, in the medium proper to a painter; that is, he made it visible. But when he attempted to voice an explanation of what he had achieved and of what was projected, he fell back on an inadequate ontic theory inherited from his broader cultural tradition. As a theorist of his own medium, he was unable to overcome the attitude in which the priority is given to conceptual constructions, and to natural science's mathematical formulations, for an interpretation of the "real" world. No modern Frenchman easily escapes the burden of Descartes. Nor does any modern individual easily suspend the intellectual legacy of Euclid and Galileo.

Nor, for that matter, can any contemporary individual archly continue to ignore the insights of recent phenomenologists to relieve us of these burdens. On a phenomenological interpretation, it is clear that when Cézanne turned to his primary work, to his brushes and pigments and his own visual experience, he overcame the inadequate conceptual model that disrupted his efforts to explain that work. In the practice of his art he "knew" that he was representing the original emergence of Nature into its being a world wherein a man dwells spatially. In that practice, he followed his own advice, written to a young painter: "we must render the image of what we see, forgetting everything that existed before us."[30] Yet when his contemporaries did not see the realism of what he presented, and when he could not explain it verbally, he was led to suspect even his own eyesight.

From our perspective, this is a particularly interesting dilemma, because if Cézanne had been less of a theoretically engaged intelligence, like Van Gogh or Matisse for example, he would have escaped this inner conflict, but then, his painting would have lacked that essential component of "logical intensity," and he would not have been the painter of *Mont Sainte-Victoire.*

In this respect, Cézanne's doubt exhibits the perennial condition of the creative artist, even if the conflict may be evaded in some instances by a suppression of intellectual engagement. His resolute persistence—what Heidegger would call *Entschlossenheit*—in the face of continuing disparagement from others and his own tormenting personal uncertainty comes to stand as a symbol for creative expression. An artist's expressive act is fulfilled only when his prior understanding is set forth in his work; but if only he can see it there, then the possibility remains that he is imposing a significance on his work that has not been brought to concrete expression.

On the other hand, because a work of creative expression institutes a new significance and establishes a new meaning horizon whose own structure provides the only appropriate norm for its interpretation, it may be the case—as history has proved it was with Cézanne's paintings—that one audience remains too committed to its established interpretive scheme, of what is real and what the artist's task is, to see what lies there before its very eyes. The artist can only offer the results of his best efforts, but for his works to mediate an experience of communication, the cooperation of a genuinely open percipient is required.

Finally, creative expression can arise only on the ground of the artist's own understanding, and because he is a historical being this will be an understanding of a world that has been previously interpreted in the expressions of his predecessors. His new interpretation must speak understandably to others, whose own perspective will have been determined, for the most part, by an inherited tradition. When he breaks new ground, he does so with no guarantee that his act will result in significant communication. He can only live, then, in the uncertainty that characterizes the condition of a being who projects his future on the basis of his past, and who performs the acts judged in the present to lead toward that anticipated resolution. But when his life and his works exhibit the full structure of this existential condition, he may stand as a clarifying example of the situation each of us is in. And the single example of Cézanne's case may yield eidetic insight into the basic condition of a being-in-the-world committed to expressing a genuine understanding of the primary significances of that condition.

If the ontological turn laid out in Heidegger's philosophical discourse enables us to resolve the dilemma posed by Cézanne's doubt concerning his own creativity, that same discourse exhibits all the characteristics to be found in any act of creative expression. It constitutes for us the last significant locus for examining this phenomenon. To show the relationship between the originary expressions of artists and the secondary expressions of scientific theorists is no mean feat; it requires an ontological explanation of how human beings interpret the significance of their personal worlds.

Our search, then, for a primal, shared meaning horizon that makes possible acts of communication began with the abstract, purely conceptual, and mathematized universe of Galilean Nature, only to move to the personally experienced "life-world" of Husserlian phenomenology, and eventually to the unitary significance Heidegger called "worldhood"—the structure of our own existence as human beings that is always already understood whenever a human existent dwells understandingly in its natural and cultural region.

The subsequent focus on perceptual experience, suggested by Merleau-Ponty's thesis of the "primacy of perception," permitted a primary expression of intuitive significance to be illustrated in Cézanne's artistic presentation of how our spatiality looks. The creative act of the painter, as a *corps-sujet* actively engaged in animating his significant situation, demonstrates how the prior ontological understanding of one's own being-in-the-world may be brought to originary expression in an artifact that interprets for us all our placement in a shared space and thereby makes communally accessible the personal experience that gives meaning to the abstract concept of "space" inherited by Galileo from pure geometry.

With this example of authentic expression, we bring to full circle the projected task of tracing available concepts, the *gedacht*, to their origins in acts of creative expression, the *gedichtet*, and back once again into the complex context where concepts meaningfully articulate the world we all live in and, in some way, understand as the meaning horizon that underlies all our efforts to communicate.

CHAPTER 7

Conclusion: Creativity in Art, Science, and Philosophy

Nietzsche's dictum asserting the priority of what has been "*gedichtet*" with respect to what can be "*gedacht*" is itself a creative expression of a philosophical idea. It is an interpretation of the origin of all concepts, hence of the ground for all thought, and for all communication: those human acts in which a significance is inventively established. But his saying, no less than any other, requires interpretation if the understanding it expresses is to be made our own. The full significance of his idea becomes explicit only when we have brought to light the structures of human existence that make possible such acts of creative expression, including Nietzsche's own, and indeed only when those acts are seen to be an authentic manner of interpreting the world wherein a human being lives.

In my own effort to understand these structures, the fertile development within the recent phenomenological tradition—from Husserl's transcendental philosophy, through Merleau-Ponty's existential anthropology, to Heidegger's fundamental ontology—has emerged as the achievement of a radically grounded account of the creative acts Nietzsche identified as the source of all concepts. And Nietzsche's idea, in turn, has emerged as the significance uniting the efforts of these three philosophers into a single project. In their desire to revitalize the vocation of philosophy by restoring to it the primordial contact with actual human lives, they were guided by the Nietzschean insight whereby such life is seen to be that out of which, as well as that for the sake of which, philosophical reflection is performed.

From this perspective, the ontic activity understood as creative expression, whether executed by scientists, artists, or philosophers, is seen to have its possibility, as well as its inherent norms, rooted in the ontological structures of human existence, and ultimately in the basic condition Heidegger called "Being-in-the-world." When an expressive act is performed that brings the significance of one's personal world into the light of a mutual understanding, so as to communicate to others how it is to exist in the "one world" wherein we all dwell together, a unitary ontic-ontological structure is implicated: the structure I have called "creativity." Gestures are performed in space and time, directed by the anticipatory understanding that will be expressed in those same gestures as their significance; as a result, an expressive artifact is created, exhibiting in its own phenomenal structures the significance of a world; it thereby mediates the mutual being-toward a world that underlies the shared meaning horizon presupposed by all communication. Such is the task, and the achievement, of creative expression.

When creativity is understood as an ontic-ontological structure that belongs to each human existent as a possibility rooted in its own being in the world, the paradox of creative expression will be resolved in theory even as it has already been resolved in practice by creative artists. Heidegger's analysis may enable us to see how the structure of human existence exhibits a prior understanding of the significance belonging to whatever worlds may have been disclosed in the personal act of finding oneself in the opening of a surrounding region. This understanding of the worldhood wherein one's possibilities are projected is itself based on the temporal stretch by which any human existent is "ahead of" itself, that is, always already dwelling in a world understandingly. Any actual human being is always equipped with a past, projecting a future, and animating that immediate region within which it is alongside entities in the present. Human existence is historical existence; it is temporal; and it is spatial.

This ontological interpretation of the existential structures of human being is the basis on which I have attempted to elucidate the phenomenon of creative expression. The aim of my phenomenological inquiry has been to make clear how historical human acts, rooted in authentic "self-possession" and the concomitant "possession" of a world, have inventively brought forth into the realm of communal understanding the meanings and meaning horizons that are characteristic of distinctively modern culture. Because "secondary expressions," or "idle talk," function with their proper and empirically evident effectiveness only on the presupposed ground of just such a shared understanding, the focus on epochal acts of genuinely creative expression also elucidate the ground of everyday talk.

Because scientific thought, and specifically mathematical physics, most clearly manifests the forgetfulness of human responsibility for inventively establishing the required contexts for any communication, and because it most forcefully presents the crisis of creativity facing modern culture, the origin of the scientific concept of Nature as represented by the texts of Galileo was first examined in order to see how the contemporary understanding of our natural environment has been articulated. As a result of commencing with Galileo's persuasive synthesizing of physical nature and the ideal science of geometry, "space" came to be the exemplary concept whose origin was to be elucidated.

First through Husserl's critique of Galilean science, and then through Heidegger's own creative advancement of his mentor's insights, it has become clear that the priority traditionally given to ontic descriptions over ontological interpretation must be reversed, if indeed the genuine foundation of the conception of nature as a spatial world is to be clarified.

Husserl showed that science's conceptual constructions must be grounded in the horizon of a "life-world"; Heidegger, that this horizon is grasped first as the ontological structure he called "worldhood," a structural component of human existence with which anyone is already familiar insofar as it is the significant region wherein he dwells.

In particular, according to Heidegger, spatiality is the ontological structure understood a priori in any dealing with entities in the life-world, as the region of possibility for all bodily movement. On the basis of this personally felt significance, the act of spatializing one's world may also be brought to primary expression in various modes of communication, so as to make available a communal understanding of the spatiality presupposed in Galileo's quantification of space.

It is now clear that the import of Galileo's famous metaphor—that a scientist's task is to read the book of Nature—implicates his own prior understanding of his own being-in-the-world: he had in advance his own physical engagement in his life-world; out of this he fore-sighted the abstract place-relations of entities in their physical being; and he fore-conceived the totality of this abstraction in terms of space, as interpreted by Euclidean geometry. The "fore-structure" of this understanding was brought to concrete expression in the poetic, and prescientific, image of "a book" written in the language of mathematics. But space, as expressed in Galileo's metaphor, remains an abstract concept; hence a grounded understanding of it requires a basis in some primary experience of its significance.

In search of just such an experience, I turned to a primary expression of personally experienced significance in the second phase of this inquiry. Cézanne's act of painting was found to present directly to our "perceptual consciousness" the expressive result of his own spatializing of his world, and indeed of our own insofar as we submit to the visual experience of his art in a moment of cooperation with the painter's efforts. His *Mont Sainte-Victoire* enables us to feel the tensions that constitute the perceptual act of spatializing, in which a vicinity originally emerges spanning far and near. In this personal experience we are directed away from the here, where we are placed when we see, toward a there, where entities are aligned significantly, in this case as a result of Cézanne's modulations of colors into the three rising planes of his abstract design. And because the structure of our own spatiality is made visible in this act of the artist, it may be shared by anyone who would see how the objects of vision are brought to a vibrant existence within the space created in the painting.

Merleau-Ponty's analysis of this primary act of expression brought to clarity the fundamental role of the living body in this "birth of knowledge" and revealed one of the reasons for the primacy of perception in our knowledge of the "external" world. We know that the perceived world is actual, and indeed spatial, because perception is felt as a tension in the living body, which itself is spatial, as it constantly restructures itself in response to the summons of the perceptual situation in which objects and the world perpetually intrude on its equilibrium from afar, even while they escape a fully transparent disclosure. In "living my body," as Merleau-Ponty puts it, I am stretched into contact with a spatial world, and this nonreflective engagement in a transcendent world unites reflective consciousness with its ontic situation. Cézanne's act of painting, interpreted by Merleau-Ponty, presents us with a primary expression of "space" by showing us how it looks when the inherited and abstract conceptual explanations of physicalistic objectivism have been "bracketed" out and we see for ourselves the world given to our own primary experience.

Yet the crisis of Cézanne's doubt concerning his own creativity left a dilemma unresolved by Merleau-Ponty. Neither the painter nor the philosopher was able to account for the evident unity of "eye" and "mind" necessarily implicated by the painter's achievement: Cézanne because as a theorist he relied on the secondary expressions of natural science to convey a conceptually clearer picture of spatial reality than was given by his own "sensations of color," and Merleau-Ponty because he took a correlation between entities, that is, between the living body and its world, to be the final stand of phenomenological reduction. The theories of both Frenchmen, painter and philosopher alike, remained ontic.

Again, Heidegger's fundamental ontology showed how we could avoid the limitations that ontic analysis must always encounter. And his ontic-ontological distinction allowed us to exhibit the unity of the underlying structures needed for interpreting the significance of Cézanne's doubt. In this case "disclosedness," or the uniquely human manner of existing as "being-disclosing," served as the ontological clue for resolving the conflict between the artist's evident achievement in the practice of his primary medium and his inability to explain what he sought there when he turned to the secondary medium of linguistic expression. The resolution of this conflict exhibited the proper relation between artistic and scientific expression: artistic expression presents on the surface of our perceptual field the significance of the region to which we are open in primary experience, whereas scientific expression abstracts from this experience in order to idealize and objectify nature so as to be able to think it in the universal terms of space and time, indeed as itself an object exhibiting constant and preestablished principles of order, illustrated most clearly in the case of universal causality.

What then can be said for creativity in philosophy itself? The portion of the history of philosophy treated here culminates in Heidegger's own interpretation of the human activity of making interpretations. In his existential analytic of this mode of human comportment, he demonstrated by his own expressive act the creativity presupposed in any authentic act of interpretation, and he brought this structure to explicit understanding by taking it as the theme of his philosophical discourse. In his interpretation of being-in-the-world, as the basic condition of his own existence, he realized the possibility of creatively expressing the understanding that essentially belongs to that condition. And in that act he fulfilled Nietzsche's charge to the "strongly constituted": to reverse the nihilism manifested in philosophy since Plato, and to establish man's own being as the "base on which he can invent his *higher form of being*."[1] As a being characterized by an understanding of its own being, man is charged with the responsibility for, and granted the possibility of, creatively achieving his own future; by the same stroke, he is obliged to understand the origin of concepts in his own expressive activity.

Because Heidegger performed this reversal and expressed it in the medium of philosophical discourse, he "leaped ahead" for us and opened our own possibilities for explicitly understanding and interpreting the ontic-ontological structure of creativity, which is necessarily implicated in the very act of having a spatial world.

The origin of the Galilean conception of space has been seen to lie in the act of spatializing—an act made visible by Cézanne. And this act has been seen to emerge out of our own spatiality—the ontological structure interpreted by Heidegger as an essential component of the basic condition of our existence. In turn, and after making the ontological turn, whereupon spatiality becomes explicitly understood, it is possible to interpret Cézanne's painting as a creative expression representative of the manner by which our communal world is spatialized. And on the basis of this shared understanding, the space intended by natural science functions as a significant concept.

What Heidegger has created now seems clear; it is a philosophy that opens up a way for interpreting significances as they are felt and as they are, all within the disclosedness of a continuous, historical act, brought to communicative expression within the ontic experiences of human subjects. It is for this reason no doubt that the creative genius of a Galileo, passing through the critical devices of an Edmund Husserl, may be viewed for what it was—the working out of a mathematically determined "fore-structure" of understanding; Heidegger was perhaps, as he believed, the first to make clear the ontological basis for the necessity of some fore-structure.

His own, of course, was supplied by his "pre-ontological understanding" of being-in-the-world. And to the extent that it succeeds as a truly universal methodology, this same philosophical creation allows whoever is interested in learning it to understand the anguish felt by Cézanne as he perceived the difference between the perceptual value of his paintings and the expectations set up by the conceptual values built into Western tradition by the Galilean view of nature.

Nature for nature, the scientist's and the artist's reading of the same book, both reflect what Heidegger always exploited as his own philosophical discovery—the ontic-ontological difference. What was exploited in each ontic concern, science and painting as separate intellectual disciplines, may now be viewed as two aspects of a single phenomenon: how a significance is moved from where it is felt to another context, another location, in which it is at last understood. Indeed, it is this transition, from a felt prior significance to a publicly expressed significance, executed in the creative act, that exhibits the creativity fundamental to all understanding. And, if we recall the Greek root *metapherein*, we might properly call this original, originary "transference" *living metaphor*, thereby indicating the creative act that lays the basis for all communication.

If I am permitted a final Heideggerianism and state that significance is ultimately "the whereupon of a projection," we may now lay some claim to have understood both the likenesses and the differences between artistic and scientific creation. And that is a philosophical achievement: explaining what those likenesses and differences are.

It just so happens, in Heidegger's case, that both modes of creativity have been projected upon the same context: the ontological structures of human existence that in consequence of their original implicitness make possible any understanding whatsoever.

Hence, the final mode of creativity, the philosophical, has been implicit within my own discourse from the beginning. Heidegger took his beginning from the work of Husserl only to transcend that beginning by elucidating what "existentials" are implicit in anyone's experience of a life-world. Tracing them from the *gedacht* to the *gedichtet* is merely a working out of the ontic-ontological reversal.

Let us trace it again: the criticism of science led us to philosophy, but a criticism of that philosophy led us to a criticism of art.

Our path has indeed been circular, from concepts to intuitions and back once again into a condition in which neither is empty or blind. We need only remind ourselves here of the path we have followed projecting our understanding of both concepts and percepts onto the ontological structures that have made such things understandable in the first place.

Galileo, Husserl, Heidegger constituted one moment of viable historicity. Cézanne, Merleau-Ponty, and Heidegger, another. If we were moved from one epoch in the history of science to another in the history of art, it was to make clear what had been asserted in Nietzsche's dictum:

Bevor "gedacht" wird, muss schon "gedichtet" worden sein.

Notes

Chapter 1

1. Friedrich Nietzsche, *The Will to Power,* trans. Walter Kaufmann and R. J. Hollingdale, ed. Walter Kaufmann (New York: Random House, 1967), Sec. 544.

2. Maurice Merleau-Ponty, *Phenomenology of Perception,* trans. Colin Smith (New York: The Humanities Press, 1962), 184.

3. Compare Merleau-Ponty's theory of language, for example, as presented in Chapter 6, "The Body as Expression, and Speech," *Phenomenology of Perception,* 174–99. This "circular" pattern of interpretation, of course, had already been laid out in Heidegger's *Being and Time.*

4. Martin Heidegger, *Being and Time,* trans. John Macquarrie and Edward Robinson (Oxford: Basil Blackwell, 1973).

5. Paul Ricoeur, *Husserl: An Analysis of His Phenomenology,* trans. Edward G. Ballard and Lester E. Embree (Evanston, Ill.: Northwestern University Press, 1967), 8–9.

6. Émile Bernard, *Souvenirs sur Paul Cézanne* (Paris, 1912), 114; cited in Erle Loran, *Cézanne's Composition* (Berkeley and Los Angeles: University of California Press, 1943), 131. My emphasis.

7. For a classic study of this thesis, see Herbert Read, *Icon and Idea: The Function of Art in the Development of Human Consciousness* (Cambridge, Mass.: Harvard University Press, 1955). Read provides numerous analyses of artistic images, including ancient cave paintings, to support his "general thesis, that artistic activity preceded any coherent intellectual activity," (pp. 87–88) and his underlying principle: "what has not first been created by the artist, is unthinkable by the philosopher" (p. 70).

Chapter 2

1. Galileo, *Discoveries and Opinions of Galileo,* trans. Stillman Drake (Garden City, N.Y.: Doubleday Anchor Books, 1957), 64. In a letter to B. Vinta, Duke Cosimo's secretary of state, Galileo wrote: "as to the title of my position, I desire that in addition to the title of 'mathematician' His Highness will annex that of 'philosopher'; for I may claim to have studied more years in philosophy than months in pure mathematics." Original: *Le Opere di Galileo Galilei, Edizione Nazionale,* X, 353.

2. Galileo, *Letter to the Grand Duchess Christina,* in *Discoveries and Opinions of Galileo,* 182. Hereafter, *Letter.*

3. *Letter.* In his introduction Drake calls this essay "Galileo's most carefully considered expression of his opinion on the proper relation of science to religion," 145.

4. Ibid., 203.

5. Ibid.

6. See, for example, *Letter,* 179, where Galileo writes: "Copernicus never discusses matters of religion or faith, nor does he use arguments that depend in any way upon the authority of sacred writings. . . . He stands always upon physical conclusions pertaining to the celestial motions, and deals with them by astronomical and geometrical demonstrations, founded primarily upon sense experiences and very exact observations."

7. Albert Einstein and Leopold Infeld, *The Evolution of Physics* (New York: Simon & Schuster, 1954), 9.

8. Galileo, *Dialogues Concerning Two New Sciences,* trans. Henry Crew and Alfonso de Salvio (New York: Dover Publications, 1954), 97. Hereafter, *TNS.*

9. Ibid., 136.

10. *Letter,* 210.

11. Galileo, *Dialogue Concerning the Two Chief World Systems—Ptolemaic and Copernican,* trans. Stillman Drake (Berkeley and Los Angeles: University of California Press, 1953), 53. Hereafter, *CWS.*

12. Part I, "The First Day," is especially pertinent.

13. *CWS,* 106.

14. Galileo's *perfetto* here plays on the ambiguity between its Aristotelian sense of "complete" and its seventeenth-century Ital-

ian sense of "supremely excellent." See translator's note, p. 468.

15. *CWS,* 19.

16. See, for example, *CWS,* 20.

17. *CWS,* 37.

18. Ibid., 40.

19. The "hindsight of the modern interpreter" mentioned here owes much to the works of writers such as N. R. Hanson, Thomas S. Kuhn, and Paul K. Feyerabend. For an analysis of Galileo's debate with the Aristotelians, see Paul K. Feyerabend, "Against Method," *Minnesota Studies in the Philosophy of Science,* IV, 17–130; and "Problems of Empiricism: Part II," *The Nature and Function of Scientific Theories,* ed. Robert G. Colodny (University of Pittsburgh, 1970), 275–353.

20. See, for example, Arthur W. Burks, *Chance, Cause, Reason: An Inquiry into the Nature of Scientific Evidence* (Chicago: The University of Chicago Press, 1977). In this effort to save the traditional (hypothetico-deductive) model of science, Burks develops a "unified theory of probability, causality, and induction," in which "the uniformity of nature" is one of three presuppositions unavoidably required by inductive reasoning about the natural universe.

21. For example, the dialogues published as *TNS.*

22. *The Assayer,* in *Discoveries and Opinions,* 272.

23. *TNS,* 264.

24. *The Assayer,* 328.

25. Ludwig Wittgenstein, *Tractatus Logico-Philosophicus,* trans. D. F. Pears and B. F. McGuinness (London: Routledge and Kegan Paul, 1961).

26. Ludwig Wittgenstein, *Philosophical Investigations,* trans. G. E. M. Anscombe (New York: Macmillan Publishing Co., 1953).

27. *TNS,* 3.

28. *TNS,* 52.

29. *TNS,* 53. The practice is that of goldsmiths who apply several thicknesses of gold leaf to a short wire, then draw its length out, thereby reducing the thickness of the plate by a coefficient Galileo says can be determined geometrically because the surface of the cylindrical wire is altered in proportion to the change of length, assuming no change in quantity of matter (that is, volume) and disregarding the end surfaces.

30. *TNS,* 113. For instance, a lever, whose own weight enters into its use but is not so apparent when the lever is represented by a line of proportional length.

31. *TNS,* 251.

32. *TNS,* 178.

33. *TNS,* 276.

34. *TNS,* 276.

35. Edmund Husserl, *The Crisis of European Sciences and Transcendental Phenomenology,* trans. David Carr (Evanston, Ill.: The Northwestern University Press, 1970), see especially Sec. 9-e, "The verificational character of natural science's fundamental hypothesis," 41–43. Hereafter, *Crisis.*

36. *Crisis,* see especially Sec. 14, 68–70.

37. Nietzsche, *The Will to Power,* Sec. 767.

38. This faith was kept alive during the Middle Ages by the availability of Plato's rather Pythagorean *Timaeus* and revitalized in fifteenth-century Florence by Neo-Platonists such as Pico della Mirandola. See, for example, his *On the Dignity of Man,* trans. Charles G. Wallis (Indianapolis: Bobbs-Merrill, 1965).

Chapter 3

1. *Crisis,* 61.

2. I follow David Carr's practice in this translation of "*Geisteswissenschaften*" as "humanistic disciplines." See *Crisis,* 4, n. 2.

3. Presented before the Vienna Cultural Society on 7 and 10 May 1935, with the original title "Philosophy in the Crisis of European Mankind." It appears as Appendix I, "The Vienna Lecture," in *Crisis,* 269–99.

4. *Crisis,* 17.

5. *Crisis,* 274.

6. *Crisis,* 290.

7. *Ideas: General Introduction to Pure Phenomenology,* trans. W. R. Boyce Gibson (New York: Macmillan Publishing Co., 1962). *Cartesian Meditations: An Introduction to Phenomenology,* trans. Dorion Cairns (The Hague: Martinus Nijhoff, 1977).

8. This work, according to the translator's introduction, was written between 1934 and 1937. The following quotation is from Husserl's preface to the text published in *Philosophia;* compare *Crisis,* translator's note, 3, no. 1.

9. The following account draws primarily on "The Origin of Geometry," as published in *Crisis,* App. VI, 353–78.

10. *Crisis,* 348.

11. Ibid., 343.

12. Ibid., 346.

13. Ibid., 347.

14. Ibid., 349.

15. Ibid., 118.

16. Ibid., 127.

17. Ibid., 118.

18. Ibid., 114.

19. Ibid., 115–16.

20. Ibid., 119.

21. See, for example, Charles W. Harvey, *Husserl's Phenomenology and the Foundations of Natural Science,* unpublished dissertation, Florida State University, 1983. A revised version of this work is forthcoming from Ohio University Press's Series in Continental Thought.

22. *Crisis,* 156.

23. Ibid., 127.

24. Ibid., 51. Husserl's emphasis.

25. See my epigraph and Chapter 1, 10–11.

26. *Crisis,* 167.

27. Ibid., 168.

28. Ibid., 169.

29. Ibid.

30. Ibid.

31. *Vorlesungen zur Phänomenologie des inneren Zeitbewusstseins* (1905–1910), ed. M. Heidegger (Halle: no pub., 1928). English translation by J. S. Churchill, *The Phenomenology of Internal Time-Consciousness* (Bloomington: no pub., 1964).

32. Wittgenstein, *Tractatus.*

Chapter 4

1. Heidegger, *Being and Time,* Sec. 14, 91–95.

2. Ibid., Sec. 12, 78–86.

3. Ibid., Sec. 19, 91–95.

4. See, for example, Norwood R. Hanson, *The Concept of the Positron* (Cambridge: University Press, 1963), especially Chaps. IV and VII, where Hanson describes the uncertainty relations "as *the* conceptual foundation stone of quantum theory."

5. See, for example, Paul A. M. Dirac, *The Principles of Quantum Mechanics* (Oxford: Clarendon Press, 1958), Chap. I. The "meaning horizon" of quantum physics deserves study as the result of a creative achievement in its own right, although one that retains the central Galilean conception of a correspondence between mathematic ideality and "physical nature." Such a study, however, lies beyond my present concerns with the expression and understanding of the "space" of the life-world.

6. See, for example, Rudolph Carnap, *Die Logische Aufbau der Welt (The Logical Structure of the World),* trans. Rolf A. George (Berkeley: University of California Press, 1967).

7. *Being and Time,* 98.

8. Ibid., 120.

9. See *Vom Wesen des Grundes* (Frankfurt am Main: V. Klostermann, 1955).

10. *Being and Time,* 93.

11. Ibid., 97. It is, perhaps, worth pointing out here that Heidegger's term, like its translation, is a collective noun and its use stresses the essential interrelatedness of such entities.

12. Ibid., 93.

13. Ibid., Chap. V, Sec. A, 172–210.

14. Husserl was at work on *Crisis* from 1934 until his terminal illness in 1937 (see translator's introduction to *Crisis*); *Sein und Zeit* was first published in Husserl's *Jahrbuch* in spring 1927.

15. See *Crisis,* Sec. 49, 167.

16. See *Crisis,* Sec. 46; also Secs. 41, 44.

17. It is perhaps worth noting that, although Heidegger's *Daseinsanalytik* clearly is directed to human being, the (logical) extension of his central noun is not necessarily restricted to *Homo sapiens*; we obviously satisfy the term, and within our own tradition no other empirically known species does so.

18. *Being and Time,* 49.

19. Ibid., 49–63.

20. Ibid., 50. Heidegger's emphasis.

21. Ibid., 51. Heidegger's emphasis.

22. Ibid., 56.

23. Ibid. Heidegger's emphasis.

24. Ibid., 58.

25. Ibid. Heidegger's emphasis.

26. Ibid.

27. Ibid.

28. Ibid., 49.

29. *Über den Humanismus* (Frankfurt am Main: V. Klostermann, 1946), 19, 29.

30. By *Heideggerian phenomenology* I refer to what is worked out in *Being and Time* as published. I am aware, of course, that a "second half" was promised, and that the total project described in the introduction is directed toward the question of the meaning of Being in general. But I take Heidegger at his word when, in his preface to the seventh German edition, he says "the second half could no longer be added unless the first were to be presented anew." Thus, I speak only of the text as we have it, originally labeled "First Half."

For a detailed study of *Being and Time* in which it is argued that Heidegger's method of *Daseinsanalysis* must come to an end short of the question of the meaning of "Being in general," see Eugene F. Kaelin, *Heidegger's Being and Time: A Reading for Readers* (Tallahassee: Florida State University Press, 1988).

31. Compare Martin Heidegger, *The Basic Problems of Phenomenology,* trans. Albert Hofstadter (Bloomington: Indiana University Press, 1982), introduction, 1–24.

32. *Being and Time,* 62.

33. Ibid. Heidegger's emphasis.

34. Compare *The Basic Problems of Phenomenology,* introduction.

35. *Being and Time,* 121.

36. Ibid., 70. I can find no benefit to Macquarrie and Robinson's Latinate *existentialia,* so I shall opt for a simply constructed English noun on the model of Heidegger's German construction: "existentials."

37. Compare *The Basic Problems of Phenomenology,* especially Chap. III, 122–76.

Chapter 5

1. *Crisis,* especially Sec. 9, "Galileo's Mathematization of Nature," 23–59, and "The Origin of Geometry," Appendix VI, 353–78. The quotation is from p. 51. Husserl's emphasis.

2. Maurice Merleau-Ponty, "Eye and Mind," *The Primacy of Perception and Other Essays,* ed. James M. Edie, trans. Carleton Dallery (Evanston, Ill.: The Northwestern University Press, 1964), 159, Pt. II, Chap. 5.

3. Recent art-historical literature is strikingly unanimous on the degree of Cézanne's influence; the questions of interest have turned to the particular avenues of his impact. See, for example, the carefully documented discussion of his influence on the first generation of twentieth-century painters, that is, the pioneer Fauvists and Cubists such as Matisse, Derain, Picasso, Braque, and Leger, during the first decade of this century, in William Rubin, "Cézanne and the Beginnings of Cubism," *Cézanne: The Late Work,* ed. William Rubin (New York: The Museum of Modern Art, 1977), 151–202. In the same volume, Liliane Brion-Guerry's "The Elusive Goal" examines Cézanne's "dismantling of space," which she describes as "overturning an order that had lasted for four centuries of Western painting" (p. 73). In her words, Cézanne marks "the great divide" in the history of spatial composition.

4. Maurice Merleau-Ponty, "Cézanne's Doubt," *Sense and Non-sense,* trans. Hubert L. Dreyfus and Patricia Allen Dreyfus (Evanston, Ill.: The Northwestern University Press, 1964), 12, Pt. I, Chap. 1. Merleau-Ponty cites conversations between the painter and Émile Bernard, who published them in *Souvenirs sur Paul Cézanne* (Paris: R. G. Michel, 1912).

5. Paul Cézanne, *Letters,* ed. John Rewald, trans. Marguerite Kay, 4th ed. (New York: Hacker Art Books, 1976), 330, to Émile Bernard, 21 September 1906.

6. See the classic study by Erle Loran, *Cézanne's Composition: Analysis of His Form with Diagrams and Photographs of His Motifs* (Berkeley and Los Angeles: University of California Press, 1943). Loran treats as evident Cézanne's "failure to work out an intellectual theory coinciding with his creative productions" and offers, briefly, a psychological explanation for the conflict.

The abstract art of Picasso and Braque is representative of the departure from "reading Nature."

7. Paul Cézanne, *Mont Sainte-Victoire Seen from Les Lauves,* 1902–1904, oil on canvas, 27½″ by 35¼″. The Philadelphia Museum of Art: George W. Elkins Collection.

8. *Letters,* 316, to E. Bernard, 23 October 1905.

9. This remarkable parallel, between the painter's and the phenomenologist's methods for focusing on what is at issue in their respective endeavors, has received little attention, so far as I can determine, in the recent literature of either art theory or philosophical studies. Three exceptions, all of a phenomenological bent, may be noted.

(a) Forest Williams, "Cézanne and French Phenomenology," *Journal of Aesthetics and Art Criticism* 12, no. 4 (June 1954): 481–92. In this self-described exploratory essay, Williams considers the "possibility of a thematic connection between a great artist [Cézanne] and a philosophical development [French phenomenology]," namely an implementation in each case of the same "distinctive capacity of human consciousness for the exclusive purpose of discovering *the appearing reality.*" He explicitly identifies "the famous method of 'reduction' [as the means] by which the character of the given is brought reflectively to full evidence and its essential or 'eidetic' structure seen." And yet he suggests—cautiously but nevertheless inexplicably—that the movement shared by painter and phenomenologist "is a return to the pre-modern and pre-baroque objectivity of the Renaissance, i.e., a return to a classical outlook."

(b) Charles W. Harvey, "A Note on the Existential Foundations of Phenomenological Reduction," *The Journal of the British Society for Phenomenology* 17, no. 2 (May 1986): 193–97. In this brief discussion by a writer who is aware that the proper "phenomenological return" is to the life-world of the reflecting subject, Harvey argues for recognizing "the proto-methodological structure and the 'naturalistic' occurrence of epoché, reduction, and constitution" in those striking moments within "natural experience" when we are "taken aback." He thus offers, albeit briefly, a theoretical framework for the parallel between phenomenological *epoché* and Cézanne's "forgetting" that I have pointed out.

(c) Eugene F. Kaelin, *Art and Existence* (Lewisburg, Pa.: Bucknell University Press, 1970). Here and in numerous articles Kaelin presents a fully developed phenomenological aesthetics in which a consciously applied "bracketing" is the first methodological step for isolating an artwork as a significant phenomenal structure whose intrinsic values will then govern any given aesthetic experience of it; the practice of *epoché* determines the expressive context, and the field of evidence, relevant for any art-critical discourse. My reading of *Mont Sainte-Victoire* represents an application of just such an approach.

10. *Letters,* 306, to E. Bernard, 25 July 1904.

11. *Letters,* 315, to E. Bernard, Friday 1905.

12. *Letters,* 261, to Joachim Gasquet, 26 September 1897.

13. *Letters,* 303, to E. Bernard, 26 May 1904.

14. Émile Bernard, "Paul Cézanne," *L'Occident* (July 1904): 23–25. Cited by Lawrence Gowing in "The Logic of Organized Sensations," *Cézanne: The Late Work,* ed. William Rubin (New York: The Museum of Modern Art, 1977), 57.

15. "Cézanne's Doubt," 18.

16. *Letters,* 327, to his son, 8 September 1906.

17. E. Bernard, "Paul Cézanne," cited by L. Gowing, "The Logic of Organized Sensations," 62. See n. 14.

18. "Cézanne's Doubt" first appeared in *Fontaine,* no. 47 (December 1945). "Eye and Mind" was the last work Merleau-Ponty saw published. It appeared in the inaugural issue of *Art de France,* 1, no. 1 (January 1961).

19. "Cézanne's Doubt," 19.

20. Ibid.

21. Ibid.

22. Ibid.

23. Ibid.

24. Ibid., 18.

25. Ibid., 20.

26. Originally published as *Phénoménologie de la Perception* (Paris: Gallimard, 1945).

27. Merleau-Ponty, "The Primacy of Perception and Its Philosophical Consequences," *The Primacy of Perception and Other Essays,* trans. James M. Edie (Evanston, Ill.: The Northwestern University Press, 1964), 25, Pt. I, Chap. 2.

28. Ibid.

29. Immanuel Kant, *Critique of Pure Reason,* trans. Norman Kemp Smith (New York: St. Martin's Press, 1965), A 51, B 75.

30. "Primacy of Perception," 17.

31. Ibid., 25.

32. Ibid.

33. Ibid., 16.

34. *Signs,* trans. R. C. McCleary (Evanston, Ill.: The Northwestern University Press, 1964), 20–21. Translation slightly modified.

35. *Letters,* 327, to his son, 8 September 1906.

36. "Cézanne's Doubt," 15. Merleau-Ponty's emphasis.

37. Ibid.

38. See, for example, *Ideas,* Sec. 135, "Object and Consciousness: Transition to the Phenomenology of Reason," 345–49.

Chapter 6

1. Merleau-Ponty, *Phenomenology of Perception,* 190. Compare his theory of the origin of language, that is, the source of authentic speech, in a *corps-sujet,* an embodied subject, in Chap. 6, "The Body as Expression, and Speech," 174–99.

2. Husserl, *The Crisis of European Sciences and Transcendental Phenomenology.* See especially Sec. 9, "Galileo's mathematization of nature," 23–59; Appendix II, "Idealization and the Science of Reality—The Mathematization of Nature," 301-14; Appendix VI, "The Origin of Geometry," 353–78.

3. *Crisis,* Sec. 9 and Appendix VI.

4. Merleau-Ponty, *The Structure of Behavior,* trans. Alden L. Fisher (Boston: Beacon Press, 1963); originally published in French under the title *La Structure du Comportement* (Paris: Presses Universitaires de France, 1942).

5. Ibid., 210: "the notions of soul and body must be relativized: there is the body as mass of chemical components in interaction, the body as dialectic of living being and its biological milieu, and the body as dialectic of social subject and his group; even all our habits are an impalpable body for the ego of each moment. Each of these degrees is soul with respect to the preceding one, body with respect to the following one."

6. *Phenomenology of Perception,* 351.

7. "Primacy of Perception," 51; *Phenomenology of Perception,* 146.

8. "Primacy of Perception," 22–23.

9. *Phenomenology of Perception,* 78–79. Like Heidegger, Merleau-Ponty was quite careful in his selection of prepositions; his choice of *au* in *l'être-au-monde* should not be obscured by translating this term into the same English term that is appropriate for Heidegger's *In-der-Welt-sein.*

10. See Chapter 3, pp. 57–58.

11. See, for example, his "Eye and Mind" and the working notes published as *Le Visible et l'invisible,* in *Bibliotheque des Idées* (Paris: Gallimard, 1964), text prepared by Claude Lefort; English translation by A. Lingis, *The Visible and the Invisible* (Evanston, Ill.: The Northwestern University Press, 1964). A note in the latter, from February 1959, speaks of "the necessity of bringing the results of the *Phenomenology of Perception* to ontological explicitation" (p. 153 in English edition; p. 237 in French edition).

For two perceptive studies of Merleau-Ponty's ontological interests in his late work, see M. C. Dillon, "Merleau-Ponty and the Reversibility Thesis," *Man and World,* 16, no. 4 (1983): 365–88; and " 'Eye and Mind': The Intertwining of Vision and Thought," *Man and World,* 13, no. 2 (1980): 155–71.

12. "Eye and Mind," 181.

13. See Chapter 3.

14. As previously, in Chapter 4, the English *existential* used as a noun translates Heidegger's *Existenzial*; it is the name given to the *explicata* appropriate for interpreting human existence-structures.

15. Heidegger, *Being and Time,* trans. John Macquarrie and Edward Robinson (Oxford: Basil Blackwell, 1973), 78.

16. *Being and Time,* 135.

17. Ibid., Sec. 23, 138–44.

18. Ibid., Chap. V, A, Secs. 29–34, 172–210. Heidegger's term is *Erschlossenheit,* which is introduced as a technical term on p. 105 (p. 75 in German edition).

19. Ibid.

20. Ibid., Sec. 29, 172–79.

21. Ibid., Sec. 31, 182–88.

22. Ibid., Sec. 34, 203–10.

23. Ibid., 184–86.

24. Ibid., 191.

25. Ibid.

26. Ibid., 189.

27. In *Being and Time* (p. 205) Heidegger writes, "In 'poetical' discourse, the communication of the existential possibilities of one's state-of-mind [*Befindlichkeit*] can become an aim in itself, and this amounts to a disclosing of existence."

In *The Basic Problems of Phenomenology,* trans. Albert Hofstadter (Bloomington: Indiana University Press, 1982), 171–72, he writes:

> What is important is only whether the human existent, in conformity with its existential possibility, is original enough still to *see* on its own the world that is always already unveiled with its existence, to verbalize it, and thereby to make it expressly visible for others. Poetry, creative literature, is nothing but the elementary emergence into words, the becoming-uncovered, of existence as being-in-the-world. For the others who before it were blind, the world first becomes visible by what is thus spoken. (Translation slightly modified. Heidegger's emphasis.)

His point is demonstrated by an immediately following lengthy quotation from Rainer Marie Rilke. And in his three lectures, *"Der Ursprung des Kunstwerkes," Holzwege* (Frankfurt-am-Main: V. Klostermann, 1950), he generalized the notion of "poetical discourse" so as to include the works of painters and temple builders. English translation by Albert Hofstadter, "The Origin of the Art Work," *Philosophies of Art and Beauty,* ed. A. Hofstadter and Richard Kuhns (New York: The Modern Library, 1964).

28. *Being and Time,* Chap. IV, 149-68.

29. *Letters,* 303, to E. Bernard, 26 May 1904.

30. *Letters,* 316, to E. Bernard, 23 October 1905.

Chapter 7

1. Friedrich Nietzsche, *The Will to Power,* Sec. 866. Nietzsche's emphasis.

Bibliography

Bernard, Émile. "Paul Cézanne." *L'Occident* (July 1904): 23–25.

______. *Souvenirs sur Paul Cézanne.* Paris: R. G. Michel, 1912.

Burks, Arthur W. *Chance, Cause, Reason: An Inquiry into the Nature of Scientific Evidence.* Chicago: The University of Chicago Press, 1967.

Carnap, Rudolph. *The Logical Structure of the World.* Trans. Rolf A. George. Berkeley: University of California Press, 1967.

Cézanne, Paul. *Letters.* Ed. John Rewald, trans. by Marguerite Kay, 4th ed. New York: Hatcher Art Books, 1976.

______. *Mont Sainte-Victoire Seen from Les Lauves.* Oil on canvas, 27½ by 35¼ inches. 1902–1904. The Philadelphia Museum of Art: George W. Elkins Collection.

Dillon, M. C. " 'Eye and Mind': The Intertwining of Vision and Thought." *Man and World,* 13, no. 2 (1980): 155–71.

______. "Merleau-Ponty and the Reversibility Thesis." *Man and World,* 16, no. 4 (1983): 365–88.

Dirac, Paul A. M. *The Principles of Quantum Mechanics.* Oxford: Clarendon Press, 1958.

Einstein, Albert, and Leopold Infeld. *The Evolution of Modern Physics.* New York: Simon & Schuster, 1954.

Feyerabend, Paul K. "Against Method." *Minnesota Studies in the Philosophy of Science,* Vol. 4, 17–130.

______. "Problems of Empiricism: Part II." *The Nature and Function of Scientific Theories.* Ed. Robert G. Colodny. Pittsburgh: University of Pittsburgh, 1970, 275–353.

Galilei, Galileo. "The Assayer." Trans. Stillman Drake. In *Discoveries and Opinions of Galileo.* Garden City, N.Y.: Doubleday Anchor Books, 1957.

———. *Dialogue Concerning the Two Chief World Systems—Ptolemaic and Copernican.* Trans. Stillman Drake. Berkeley: University of California Press, 1953.

———. *Dialogue Concerning Two New Sciences.* Trans. Henry Crew and Alfonso de Salvio. New York: Dover Publications, 1954.

———. *Le Opere di Galileo Galilei. Edizione Nazionale.* Firenze: Tipografia Barbèra, 1890–1909. 20 vol.

———. "Letter to the Grand Duchess Christina." Trans. Stillman Drake. In *Discoveries and Opinions of Galileo.* Garden City, N.Y.: Doubleday Anchor Books, 1957.

Hanson, Norwood R. *The Concept of the Positron.* Cambridge: Cambridge University Press, 1963.

Harvey, Charles W. *Husserl's Phenomenology and the Foundations of Natural Science.* Unpublished dissertation. Tallahassee: Florida State University, 1983. Revised version forthcoming from Ohio University Press, Series in Continental Thought.

———. "A Note on the Existential Foundations of Phenomenological Reduction." *The Journal of the British Society for Phenomenology,* 17, no. 2 (May 1986): 193–97.

Heidegger, Martin. *The Basic Problems of Phenomenology.* Trans. Albert Hofstadter. Bloomington: Indiana University Press, 1982.

———. *Being and Time.* Trans. John Macquarrie and Edward Robinson. Oxford: Basil Blackwell, 1973.

———. *Nietzsche, Vol. I: The Will to Power as Art.* Trans. David Farrell Krell. San Francisco: Harper & Row, 1979.

———. *Über den Humanismus.* Frankfurt-am-Main: V. Klostermann, 1946.

———. *Vom Wesen des Grundes.* Frankfurt-am-Main: V. Klostermann, 1955.

———. "Der Ursprung des Kunstwerkes." *Holzwege,* Chap. I. Frankfurt-am-Main: V. Klostermann, 1950.

———. "The Origin of the Work of Art." Trans. Albert Hofstadter. *Philosophies of Art and Beauty.* Ed. A. Hofstadter and Richard Kuhns. New York: The Modern Library, 1964, 649–701.

Husserl, Edmund. *Cartesian Meditations: An Introduction to Phenome-*

nology. Trans. Dorion Cairns. The Hague: Martinus Nijhoff, 1977.
______. *The Crisis of European Sciences and Transcendental Phenomenology*. Trans. David Carr. Evanston, Ill.: The Northwestern University Press, 1970.
______. *Ideas: General Introduction to Pure Phenomenology*. Trans. W. R. Boyce Gibson. New York: Macmillan Publishing Co., 1962.
______. *The Phenomenology of Internal Time-Consciousness*. Trans. J. S. Churchill. Bloomington : n.p., 1964.
______. *Vorlesungen zur Phänomenologie des inneren Zeitbewusstseins* (1905–1910). Ed. M. Heidegger. Halle: n.p., 1928.
______. "The Origin of Geometry." In *Crisis,* Appendix VI.
______. "The Vienna Lecture." In *Crisis,* Appendix I.
Kaelin, Eugene F. *Art and Existence*. Lewisburg, Pa.: Bucknell University Press, 1970.
______. *Heidegger's Being and Time: A Reading for Readers*. Tallahassee: Florida State University Press, 1988.
Kant, Immanuel. *Critique of Pure Reason*. Trans. Norman Kemp Smith. New York: St. Martin's Press, 1965.
Loran, Erle. *Cézanne's Composition: Analysis of His Form with Diagrams and Photographs of His Motifs*. Berkeley and Los Angeles: University of California Press, 1943.
Merleau-Ponty, Maurice. *Phenomenology of Perception*. Trans. Colin Smith. New York: The Humanities Press, 1981.
______. *Phénoménologie de la Perception*. Paris: Gallimard, 1945.
______. *Signs*. Trans. R. C. McCleary. Evanston, Ill.: The Northwestern University Press, 1964.
______. *The Structure of Behavior*. Trans. Alden L. Fisher. Boston: Beacon Press, 1963.
______. *La Structure du Comportement*. Paris: Presses Universitaires de France, 1942.
______. *The Visible and the Invisible*. Trans. A. Lingis. Evanston, Ill.: The Northwestern University Press, 1964.
______. *Le Visible et l'invisible. Bibliotheque des Idées;* text prepared by Claude Lefort. Paris: Gallimard, 1964.
______. "Cézanne's Doubt." *Sense and Non-sense,* Pt. I, Chap. 1. Trans. Hubert L. Dreyfus and Patricia Allen Dreyfus. Evanston, Ill.: The Northwestern University Press, 1964.
______. "Eye and Mind." *The Primacy of Perception and Other Essays,*

Pt. II, Chap. 5. Trans. Carleton Dallery. Ed. James M. Edie. Evanston, Ill.: The Northwestern University Press, 1964.

———. "The Primacy of Perception and Its Philosophical Consequences." *The Primacy of Perception and Other Essays,* Pt. I, Chap. 2. Trans. and ed. James M. Edie. Evanston, Ill.: The Northwestern University Press, 1964.

Nietzsche, Friedrich. *The Will to Power.* Trans. Walter Kaufmann and R. J. Hollingdale. Ed. Walter Kaufmann. New York: Random House, 1967.

Pico della Mirandola. *On the Dignity of Man.* Trans. Charles G. Wallis. Indianapolis: Bobbs Merrill, 1965.

Read, Herbert. *Icon and Idea: The Function of Art in the Development of Human Consciousness.* Cambridge, Mass.: Harvard University Press, 1955.

Ricoeur, Paul. *Husserl: An Analysis of His Phenomenology.* Trans. Edward G. Ballard and Lester E. Embree. Evanston, Ill.: The Northwestern University Press, 1967.

Rubin, William, Ed. *Cézanne: The Late Work.* New York: The Museum of Modern Art, 1977.

Williams, Forest. "Cézanne and French Phenomenology." *Journal of Aesthetics and Art Criticism,* 12, no. 4 (June 1954): 481–92.

Wittgenstein, Ludwig. *Philosophical Investigations.* Trans. G. E. M. Anscombe. New York: Macmillan Publishing Co., 1953.

———. *Tractatus Logico-Philosophicus.* Trans. D. F. Pears and B. F. McGuinness. London: Routledge and Kegan Paul, 1961.

Index